How to Find Love Mid-Life

Also by Andrea Kon

How to Survive Bereavement

How to Find Love Mid-Life

Andrea Kon

HELP YOURSELF

Copyright © 2003 by Andrea Kon

First published in Great Britain in 2003

The right of Andrea Kon to be identified as the Author
of the Work has been asserted by her in accordance
with the Copyright, Designs and Patents Act 1988.

10 9 8 7 6 5 4 3 2 1

British Library Cataloguing in Publication Data
A record for this book is available from the British Library

ISBN 0 340 86169 X

Typeset in ACaslonRegular by Avon DataSet Ltd,
Bidford-on-Avon, Warwickshire

Printed and bound in Great Britain by
Bookmarque Ltd, Croydon, Surrey

The paper and board used in this paperback are natural recyclable products
made from wood grown in sustainable forests. The manufacturing processes
conform to the environmental regulations of the country of origin.

Hodder & Stoughton
A Division of Hodder Headline Ltd
338 Euston Road
London NW1 3BH
www.madaboutbooks.com

For Peter Gordon
Who made it happen for me.

Contents

Acknowledgements

My heartfelt thanks to my husband, Peter, who not only gave me back a life filled with love after years in a lonely wilderness, but who offered so much support, encouragement and practical help with the male point of view as I struggled to research and write this book. I couldn't have done it without him.

My thanks, too, for Judith Longman, Editorial Director at Hodder and Stoughton for her enthusiasm, interest and support, and to Lorraine Keating, Suzanne Kennedy and the rest of the team who have done so much to promote its success. I hope I justify their faith in me.

Introduction

It was hitting the 'Big Five-O' that did it. My daughters connived with friends and arranged a surprise party. I was spoiled rotten with cards, gifts and even a novelty cake. Flushed with excitement, I fell into bed and fumbled beside me. What I wanted most to round off my big day was a warm cuddle and a goodnight kiss from someone I loved and who cared especially for me. But the space where my partner should have been was empty, and I never expected anyone would fill it again: I'd been widowed seven years previously. None of my friends knew any men who I found appealing, and, according to two marriage bureaux I'd approached to help me find a partner, since I didn't seem to be having much luck meeting suitable men through the so-called 'normal' social channels, I was too old for love.

That night, despite all the celebrations, I felt like an unwanted, unattractive brown-paper parcel; tatty round the edges and held together by fraying string. No amount of cosmetic adjustments could give me the one thing I yearned for. Like almost every other mid-life woman who finds herself alone after years in a long-term relationship, I wanted a partner of my own. I wanted to be half of a couple again. But

I didn't want to hook up with just anyone. I wanted a special man – a man I could love and who would love me for no better reason than I am who I am. I wanted to meet someone who would make me feel like the sexy, loving, generous, exciting and experienced woman I knew was lurking under the crumpled wrapping of my battered ego. No matter how successful you are in other areas of your life, a long period of aloneness can have a massively crushing effect on a woman's self-esteem.

It had taken several years from the time of my first husband's death before I decided that while I might be no longer in the first flush of youth, I was still full of life. I knew I had so much love to offer to the right man; I certainly didn't want to spend the rest of my life as a single.

Before widowhood, I, like so many other women of my generation, had never lived alone. I didn't go away to college or university. I married at the age of twenty and went from my parents' home straight to the home my first husband and I built together. The family grew. We were three and then four. My daughters grew up and the house was always full. There was always someone to entertain, to feed, to nurture, to love. Parents got older and needed as much care as the children. Our house had an open front door. Family and friends were constantly in and out. There were people who made a noise and a mess and kept our home alive, vigorous and vital. It bustled.

When our older daughter left for university, there was still one at home. But then, just a few weeks after my husband's death, the second flew the nest – and I insisted that she went. That was as it should be. But finding myself living alone for the first time in my life came as quite a shock. The stream of visitors was all mine now, until my daughters came home for their vacations. My visitors didn't make the noise or the mess I was used to. I came home at night and the house was entirely dark, hauntingly silent and totally empty. There was no one to share a drink with, put the supper on for, complain I was tired to or shout at because I'd had a bad day at the office. It took some getting used to and I hated every minute of it.

It's not only widows but also divorcees who may suddenly find themselves alone mid-life, wondering what on earth to do next. Many divorced people come out of a relationship feeling battle-weary, with bruised and badly battered egos, and have no idea how to start reinventing themselves in partnership mould. Other women I know have devoted their lives to caring for parents or nurturing a career and have never had a long-term partnership. As mid-life approaches, they may suddenly find themselves yearning to be half of a couple in a stable relationship. They look around and suddenly find themselves alone in a world where coupledom is the norm: holidays are priced for two people sharing a room, and singles are penalised by hefty supplements; restaurant tables are set in pairs, fours or sixes, always an even number; you may be the only single at a dinner party of coupled guests and wonder how to go about finding a lasting relationship now. And, as much as many middle-aged singles revel in their autonomy, the idea of a shared life becomes infinitely more appealing as you realise how good partnership can be. You have simply reached a point in your life where you long to have a partner. Yet career women in particular may find it hard to meet an intellectual and financial match who can offer the chemistry so essential if a relationship is to work. Figures published in the General Household Survey carried out by the Office of Population and Census in December 2002 showed that many women over fifty who put off marriage for the sake of their careers have found it harder than ever in mid-life to find a partner when they do decide they want to tie the knot.

After years of playing the mid-life mix-and-match game, I had discovered what I believe almost every other mature single woman who has tried it finds. Searching for 'that special someone' when you are in your forties or fifties bears no resemblance to the sport of dating and mating that people play in earlier life. As former Cabinet minister Jonathan Aitken, who announced his engagement to actress Elizabeth Harris at the end of 2002, says: 'In a late marriage, love is just as passionate as it was in the teens and twenties, but it can be a lot less blind, especially when it comes to seeing the importance of friendship between husband and wife. For happy are the marriage partners who become each other's best friends.' He was speaking from the standpoint of experience. He and Elizabeth have known one another for almost four decades. They had a passionate affair when both were married to other people back in the 1970s. Then they drifted apart.

As a middle-aged newly single person, you may find yourself in huge demand at parties to amuse happily partnered fellow guests with anecdotes of your singledom experiences. But however much laughter surrounds you, you still go back to an empty home, and even if you still share that home with your children, there's a vital component missing. When you shut the front door, you have no peer conversation, even about something as mundane as the weather. In earlier life, there was always someone else to share experiences with. 'Guess what he *said* to me last night, you'll never believe what he told me . . .' But as the years pass, the conversation with your friends has changed. If you share your experience with marrieds, they may think you're mad – or fibbing.

When you are years past the pubbing and clubbing scene, where on earth do you go to meet a potential mate? Like many others, I soon discovered that despite all the assurances that 'you're bound to find someone', friends are rarely able to introduce you to a sexy, loving, intelligent, compatible, suitable partner (with g.s.o.h. – good sense of humour); conventional marriage bureaux (certainly in the south of England) consider any woman over the age of forty 'too old'. I soon discovered that the likelihood of meeting an acceptable date by conventional means was about as likely as being offered a skiing trip to the moon and getting back before breakfast. My friends told me that 'everyone' said I should be out socialising. But where? It was winter and I certainly didn't fancy freezing on a park bench as I waited for my 'Mr Right' to appear on his white charger and whisk me away to the Land-of-Happy-Ever-After. I've never been a pubber or clubber. I was too young for the over-sixties clubs, but too old for the discos frequented by my daughters and their friends.

Working full time, I was often too tired in the evenings to think of hitting the night-school scene. I didn't know where to find suitable singles clubs – and when I did, I decided that the people who went to the ones I tried weren't 'my type'. I dated some very pleasant (and some extremely unpleasant) gentlemen along the way, but there were no instant, overwhelming physical or emotional attractions – not until many years down the line, when I met the man to whom I'm now happily married. When I went on these dates, perhaps the biggest problem was that I had no idea how to behave. Many couples who've been parted by death or divorce 'grew up' together. We were the generation that married in our late teens or early twenties in the 1960s and 1970s. We knew what to expect from one another. It may not always have been a pleasant expectation but, nevertheless, you knew one another so well that you could pre-empt sticky situations. You were comfortable in one another's company. Best friends, perhaps. So what happens when your partner is a total stranger, someone with whom you share no history? How can you get out of singledom/old-partner mould and start a fresh relationship in the middle of life? You may find the idea of going out with a member of the opposite sex, looking for all the world as though you are half of a couple, appealing. It's 'normal'. Yet that very first date with a stranger can be a frightening experience when it happens, particularly when it's your first date for twenty or even thirty years. What do you say? How much dare you reveal of yourself and how much should you be on your guard?

A major problem, I soon discovered, is the 'age' thing. Statistics in both the UK and USA prove, as we see later, a suspicion aroused in many mid-life women who want to start dating again. It's not just a myth; it's a fact that there are far more middle-aged and older women seeking partners now than at any other time in history, and they outnumber the available similarly aged men on a ratio of approximately 8:1.

The older you are, and the longer you've been alone, the harder it may be to 'open up' to a dating partner and develop an emotionally intimate relationship. Much research has been done on the subject. It's my own belief that most people who are looking for love mid-life are searching for the kind of love they've known in the past, instead of opening their hearts and minds to entirely new vistas of companionship and love. It's about giving off – and being open to receiving – the right signals from a member of the opposite sex and as you get older, there's no doubt that you get out of practice.

It's not only us ordinary folk who encounter the problem. It happens to the rich and famous, the brains and the 'bodies' too. Film star Andie MacDowell, the beautiful 'face' of l'Oreal who starred as a school headmistress in *Crush* as one of three forty-something women desperately seeking men, told Cassandra Jardine of the *Daily Telegraph* that when she read the script, she 'knew every moment'. She had just divorced her husband and admits she was 'real lonely' as a single mother living with three children. 'The dating process at forty is just awful,' she told Jardine. 'What do you do? You don't want to go to bars, so how do you find a decent person? And you don't want sex for the sake of sex, you want a relationship.' In the film, her character hits the bottle to drown her sorrows. MacDowell admits she took up smoking to console herself. 'It's bizarre to start as a woman of forty, but cigarettes were absolutely fabulous,' she says. The trouble was that she was terrified that her 'sin' would be discovered and started drowning herself in perfume to disguise the smell. Then she found herself fighting a nicotine addiction, which she claims led to rows with her offspring. She went through two years of what she describes as 'dating prospective life mates' before finding true love with 'the boy next door'. Rhett Hartzog, who she describes as a 'true Southern gentleman', had been to school with her (he now runs a jewellery business from Atlanta in the USA) and was still single. She hated the 'dating' game and one of her sisters arranged a meeting for lucky Andie: it had the proverbial 'happy fairy-tale' ending we all yearn for. They married recently and are set for a great future together. Sadly it doesn't happen that way for everyone.

The rules of mating have changed as dramatically as the rules of meeting since the last time most of us went dating, back in the heady sixties and seventies. Where do you draw the line when you're clearly no longer a virgin? Are you 'gagging for it' as many of the men you meet may believe you must be, if you've been alone and obviously celibate for some time? So-called 'free love' may have been all the rage when you were last single. The Pill offered women the first real sexual parity of experience in history, removing fear of pregnancy and the historical frontiers that had separated the 'good' girls from the 'bad'. In the early part of the twenty-first century, however, and possibly at a time when nature has been kind enough to remove the major obstacle to 'free sex', is the spectre of disease really as prevalent as publicity would have us believe? Is it absolutely essential for a middle-aged or older man to use a condom to prevent the spread of disease, including AIDS? And if it is, for how long, before you trust him to be disease free? If you're planning to go to bed with the man you are dating, or believe there's a very real possibility it might happen, might it be construed as offensive to carry condoms in your bag and suggest he uses them for safety's sake? And if he takes offence, do you give in or ditch him fast?

Whether you have sex or not isn't the only problem. Where do you draw the financial limits? Equal pay for equal work may still have been a long way from reality last time you went dating. Usually, the man who invited the girl on a date also expected to pay for the privilege of her company (unless both were both poor students at the time, in which case you went Dutch by mutual agreement). But who pays when you go dating now? Some believe it is perfectly acceptable for a sexy sophisticated and mature woman to pay her own way on a first date. A single male friend in his late-fifties, with whom I discussed this problem, told me that he believes that a man should always offer to pay until such time as a real friendship has been established. Middle-aged male pride can, it seems, be dented if the lady he's invited for a meal insists on paying her share when he's the one who issued the invitation. She, on the other hand, may feel he's a miserly sod if he expects her to split the bill for a coffee and a tea down to the very last penny because his tea was 5p cheaper than her coffee. How do you cope with finances when one member of a dating pair is clearly far better heeled than the other? How much financial independence should a mature woman retain?

There are other problems, too. The longer you're alone, the more selfish you become. You have certain standards. As a partnership of any kind is about compromise, how can you learn to compromise in new ways mid-life? You like making your bed a certain way; you *always* have your soup in a cup; you love slurping oranges; you're used to doing the ironing at 4 a.m. It's not easy to change habits honed over years of single life when you do find a suitable partner. You become less flexible and more set in your ways.

The issues surrounding the whole concept of mid-life dating are enormous. Those of us who embark on the mid-life search for love – whether for the first time, because so far they haven't met the man or woman with whom they can form a life-long partnership, or whether they are divorced or widowed – all share similar problems. As you progress through this book, you will learn about some of the major hurdles you are likely to face as you practise the steps of the mid-life dating dance towards matrimony (if that is what you really want). It's a complicated ritual. At times, it seems so fraught with difficulties that you may well be tempted to give up. But here I offer some suggestions, born of my own experience as well as other people's, of ways to learn to pirouette along the tightrope of middle-aged dating without bruising or breaking your heart too many times along the way – although I have to say it's bound to happen. Sometimes, of course, the amusement begins to pall. If you're bored, then you're going to the wrong places or meeting the wrong people. It's a game that may take you on an emotional seesaw. You may find yourself trying to juggle ten balls with one hand tied behind your back as you attempt to fit your existing life, which may well include quite young children, in with the demands of learning to flirt and to enjoy a new partner all over again. No matter how hard you try, you won't catch them all.

If this is a game you have been playing for a number of years without success and you are looking for tips to assist you in finding the love of your life mid-life and in maintaining a long and successful relationship, with or without the commitment of marriage, I'll do my best to help. But as God told the pauper who begged to be allowed to win the Lottery, you need to meet Him halfway and buy a ticket. If you don't go out and seek love for yourself and open the doors of possibility, no one can do it for you. Whether you are looking for a partner with whom to share the rest of your life (and if you're honest, you'll admit that this is probably your ultimate aim), or whether you wholeheartedly believe that you are currently just looking for some fun with members of the opposite sex, you need to give it a determined go.

Dating mid-life can be funny, fickle, humiliating, embarrassing and even soul-destroying. It can also be a life-enhancing experience, one that can offer huge rewards. However, it is vital to look for a *new* relationship and a *new partner* and not to seek a carbon copy of a partner you've had in the past. No two people are ever the same, and you may condemn yourself to wandering the wilderness of the single life for ever.

Whatever you do, don't compromise your standards for the sake of allaying your loneliness. That can only result in ultimate disaster. Whereas younger people are often open to manipulation by a new partner and may not yet have set standards for their life-style and expectations, by the time you hit forty, those standards and expectations are, to misappropriate a Maggie Thatcherism, 'not for turning'. Where once it was important to share every spare moment of time with your lover, by the time you hit mid-life and have spent time alone, you need 'space'. Although compromise is the cornerstone of any successful relationship, it may need to be relearned and the dance of give-and-take choreographed to new steps in a fresh, mid-life relationship.

If you are really lonely and longing for a partner, then there's no doubt that there is someone out there who is just like you, and who is seeking lasting love. It's just a matter of you finding one another.

This book will examine many issues surrounding the whole topic of dating mid-life and finding love. It will look at all the options available to single men and women who want to find compatible, loving partners. It will look at how you learn to love yourself so that others find you lovable; how to know who you are so that others can get to know the real you, it will seek out the secrets of marriage bureaux, the Internet, speed and media dating, and suggest ways in which you can turn loneliness into love. It will also examine ways in which you can make the most of yourself; let you share the intimate experiences of other, intrepid mid-life daters who've trodden the path ahead of you; offer expert advice on ways to make the best of yourself, and suggest how to build and maintain the relationship that will hopefully bring you lasting happiness. Most importantly, this book will suggest new ways in which you can become pro-active in your search for dating fun and, ultimately, love. For even though the odds may appear to be stacked ten miles high against you, mid-life dating *can* be done. You *can* fall deeply in love in later life. It may not be the same, frenzied passion you knew when you were younger, although chemistry will still be there; mid-life love is different – you fall in love in a deeper, perhaps even more sensuous, way. A fine romance can indeed be born as a result of mutual experience, respect and joy. However, there is only one person who can really make it happen and that is you yourself.

The path to mid-life love is not an easy journey, but then the path to true love often doesn't run smoothly, even in youth. Sometimes you may look at others who have travelled it successfully and wonder how they did it and why it hasn't happened yet for you. If you allow yourself to dwell on others' success and waste your energy bemoaning your own, single fate, you will almost certainly end up feeling more miserable and alone than ever. I know all about those feelings of self-doubt. I've been there. I can empathise entirely with the depression occasioned by the self-destructive sentiment that you must surely be the only person in the world who can't find long-term love and possibly a lifetime partner. 'What's wrong with me?' you may ask yourself. The answer is: 'Nothing.' You just haven't found your true soulmate, yet. But believe me, if you're dedicated to doing so, you will. It may take time – but then anything worth having is worth waiting for.

Thee is an important message to take on board in Rudyard Kipling's famous poem 'If': '. . . you can meet with triumph and disaster, and treat those two impostors just the same'. The disasters you will doubtlessly encounter along your way as you search for mid-life love are par for the course. Hopefully, you will learn to laugh at them in retrospect. I recall some awful dates: there was the man who invited me to tea at his very grand house because his daughter supposedly had flu, only when I arrived, I found myself confronted with his mother, his sister and his great-aunt Nellie, all of them gathered to give me the 'once over'. What made it worse was that I clearly failed the test because I remember finding myself crunching on his gravel driveway, the front door closed firmly behind me. I can't remember what I said to occasion that little episode! Then there was the man I dated and wanted to finish with, who wouldn't leave me alone. I asked him not to phone, so he wrote. I asked him not to write, so he stalked me, waiting for me on the corner of the road! It was horrible. There were men I couldn't fancy, and wouldn't touch with a bargepole, who dated me once and expected sex in return for dinner. But without these experiences, you can't appreciate the best times when they do finally happen. Because, despite all the downs, dating mid-life can be hilariously amusing, enormous fun, and deeply satisfying, if you permit it to be.

There's only one way to embark on the mid-life dating quest to find Mr or Ms Mature Right, and that is to look on the entire exercise as one huge adventure.

This book is for Miriam and Peter, Marilyn and Maurice, Sue and Stuart, Jackie and Bernard, Sue and Rob, and my own precious second soulmate, Peter. All of us played the mid-life dating game. We've all been lucky. We searched. We won. If we did it, you can do it, too!

1

The age thing

Almost anywhere in the world, you will discover that at any over-forties event the proportion of women to men averages about eight to one. Whether you're looking to meet a mate at a private party, a singles club or pub, at an interest group, or through an introduction service or dating agency, you will discover there are *always* far more available single women than there are men. Which beggars the question, where do men go looking for partners mid-life?

The glut of single women and serious dearth of men is a puzzle that generations of single mid-life women have queried. There's no question but that the rare, brave chaps who turn up to a singles do for those over forty have their pick of the field. As for us women? Like it or not, we face brisk and serious competition, wherever we go and whatever we try. But why? Everyone knows that men die younger than women. But even the male mortality figures fail to prove that the male population expires in vast numbers after the age of forty-five.

The conundrum can partially be answered because, in my experience, most intelligent and vaguely good-looking, employed, sexually appealing, newly single men get snapped up even before they know they are 'on the market' themselves.

This is partially the fault of happily partnered people who, on encountering one of these rare species, instantly introduces him to their closest single friend. Generally, she is a woman between ten and fifteen years younger, the friend-of-a-friend who's been let down by a real bastard of her own age, and is now seeking the emotional security and stability of the older male of our fickle species.

It would appear that the only men left in abundance are life's single male 'anoraks'. These are the middle-aged 'Barrys' who still go train-spotting and believe their mothers' offering of boiled ham and spotted dick and custard accompanied by a slice of bread and butter and a cup of tea is the only meal worth digesting! And for entertainment, read fish-and-chips and a night at the pub. If you're unlucky enough to get that close, you'll discover that they still wear liberty bodices and woolly long-johns and spend Saturday mornings digging for victory down on their allotments, just as their dads did!

OK, so forgive me for getting carried away. But it is a fact of life that for every one of us who does meet a mate mid-life, another eight single women over the age of forty-five seem to be seeking a partner. The best a middle-aged woman can hope for, it seems, is that her first appearance at a new singles venue will offer novelty value to her appeal. No matter how good or young you look, friends view you wistfully and sigh: 'If only I knew someone to introduce you to . . .' Or they may try to get a forty-something woman together with a seventy-plus man – on the basis that 'he looks much younger than he really is, honestly!'

Bestselling author Linda Grant, winner of the Orange Prize for fiction with her novel *When We Lived in Modern Times*, is still single at the age of fifty-one and seemingly as puzzled by the lack of men as everyone else. Indeed, the whole idea was the spark which ignited the inspiration for her latest novel, *Still Here*. She told Elizabeth Grice in an interview in the *Daily Telegraph*:

'Older men simply don't exist because the notion that women's sexual desirability stops around the menopause is such an absolute. One of my male contemporaries once told me that he would not dream of going out with a woman his own age. When a man is in his forties or fifties, he often expects to find a woman one or two decades his junior. And that a woman should ideally be half a man's age, plus seven years. I reacted with a mixture of amusement and fury. Oh, that's great! I thought, doing the sums in my mind while he was speaking. I'm exactly the right age for Saul Bellow, who's eighty-six, but slightly too old for Lucian Freud who's seventy-nine.'

About three years down the line after my first husband's death, everyone said I 'ought to get out and meet people'. I took them at their word and tried to enrol with a London dating agency. It was one of the most painful and embarrassing experiences I have ever had. As we ran through my details on the phone, an independent, professional working mother of two grown girls with a multitude of interests, they assured me that there were plenty of men out there all waiting with baited breath for my appearance in their lives. The fantasy lasted for less than the ten minutes it took to run through a standard questionnaire, motor insurance policy-style. Where did I live? What did I do for a living? My marital status? Children? Did I own my own home? I answered blithely – until the earth-shattering moment when they came to – shock horror – my age. At the time, I was forty-six. 'Oh no, my dear! I'm afraid you're too old,' I was told in tones generally reserved for geriatrics of eighy-five-plus who find themselves trying to book skiing trips. 'Now if you'd been in your thirties . . .' Two other London agencies did agree to take me on to their books, as a huge favour, and because, they said, I had a 'young' face, but as they were demanding vast fees upfront, and made it clear that at my grand age, they held out little hope of finding me the date of my dreams, I declined to do business with them. I was devastated, as I know others I have spoken to since have told me they were also. How hard is that on someone who is recovering from the life-shattering trauma of bereavement or divorce? In your mid-forties, you're considered 'over the hill' for love. It may be another fourteen years before you are eligible to collect a state retirement pension. Visit the cinema or a stately home and there are no concessions available for women in their mid-forties. No one offers to help you cross the road, or even offers you a seat on a bus or train! But, as I discovered, and according to many dating agencies and marriage bureaux (particularly in the south of England) who I spoke to in the course of researching this book, women in their mid-forties are considered too old to find new love.

Oddly, it would appear that this is one of those North/South divide issues, because agencies in the north of England are happy to enrol women who admit to being over forty, and what is more, they seem to have men on their books who express a real desire to meet a mature woman. Equally, women in their forties and fifties in the USA are considered perfectly acceptable as potential new partners. But must a woman whose life and work are rooted in the south of England leave home, family and work and move North, or indeed across the Atlantic, to stand a chance of embarking on a new and loving relationship? It would, again, appear that men in their forties, fifties and sixties in Southern Great Britain are, for the most part, seeking women at least ten, twenty, and sometimes thirty years their junior.

However, for some inexplicable reason, the pattern of older men seeking younger women does not follow where Internet partner-searching is concerned. Tony Rowlands, Vice-President, Global Communications at uDate, one of the world's largest Internet dating sites, says: 'There is a widely held and, in our belief, mistaken idea that older men invariably want a much younger partner. We find that real compatibility issues such as sharing the same sense of humour, number of children, education and interests are much more important when it comes to starting and developing a relationship online.'

The facts

In order to investigate the real and serious truth behind this age enigma, I decided to take a close look at the published statistics. Therein lies at least part of the answer. Some may believe that statistics can be fiddled, but not in this case. For although men outnumber women up to the age of forty-five, figures published by the British Office of Statistics show a dramatic about-turn for those aged forty-five-plus. Even allowing for the fact that women usually marry older men; that men who find themselves alone in mid-life may well seek a woman in her late twenties or early thirties; that men tend to die younger than women, and taking into account 'same sex' partnerships as well as those couples who choose to live together but are still technically single, the last available figures published in 2000 from the BOS show that in England and Wales there are huge discrepancies between the number of women registered as single and the equivalent number of men. There were 155,700 men aged between thirty-five and forty-four who were categorised as unattached, either because they had never married, were divorced, or were widowed, but there were only 126,200 women with single status in that age group. Between the ages of forty-five and sixty-four, the percentage of men to women had done a dramatic about-turn. There were 154,200 men registered as single in this age group, but 165,700 women! By the age of sixty-five or more, the differential had soared, with only 100,200 men registered as unattached against a massive 2,892,000 women. Sixty-five may be the officially designated retirement age, but in the twenty-first century, sixty-five is no age at all, and the most recent suggestion is that it should be raised to seventy for both men and women.

Statistics in the USA show a remarkable similarity. Of all older people who are known to live alone in the States, 6.5 million – that's 77 per cent – are women, according to a recent survey. Today, this total has been estimated to have risen to 13.3 million, 85 per cent being women. In a society where there are more than three times as many centenarians as there were just two decades ago, this seems to suggest that more 'silver' singles than ever before are looking for love, worldwide.

Recently, the BBC published a fascinating survey on the single life in Britain in 2002. Results showed that only 16 per cent of all single people over the age of fifty-five expect to find the relationships they think they're looking for. Tragically, and according to the same survey, 46- to 55-year-olds said they thought marriage was 'outdated' and although a 'nice idea', was not 'realistic'.

Why do men go for younger models?

Even the experts don't really seem able to offer sensible answers. Linda Davis, chairperson of the Association of British Introduction Agencies, points out:

'I can get a 65-year-old guy registering, but he's probably looking for a woman in the 55–60 age bracket. He would possibly demand a woman of fifty, if we let him, but we know it wouldn't work, from experience. Yet both men and women perceive that there should be around a ten-year age differential with men always being the older, even in the younger age groups.'

The truth of the matter is, of course, that many older men who find themselves 'off the leash' for the first time in maybe two or three decades, are out to plume their peacock feathers and incite the envy of their pals by appearing with a sexy, attractive and very young female draped on their arm. The enormous choice displayed before them can be intoxicating – and devastating news for exes already struggling to heal battered egos, only to discover that their former partners are dating women often twenty, thirty, or even forty years their junior. But as many 'sugar daddies' soon discover to their financial, intellectual and emotional cost, taking up with a much younger woman is not always the nirvana they expected. As you get older, interests, conversation and tastes change with experience. It happens to women who are gracious enough to accept that that's the way it is. It happens to men, too. Generally, however, it just takes them longer to realise it.

The trophy syndrome

Many men seem to consider that sporting a (very) young lady on their arm is in effect sporting a trophy. 'Look,' they seem to be saying, 'I may be a little wrinkled, but I can still pull 'em in.' But, of course, they're not all as clever as the older man who waltzed into a furrier with a lovely young thing on his arm: 'It's my niece's birthday and I've promised her any coat in the shop she fancies,' he said as the girl pranced around in sable and ermine, admiring herself. 'I'll write you a cheque,' he said as she settled on an outrageously expensive wrap. 'I'm afraid you can't take it with you until we clear the cheque, but you can pick it up on Monday,' said the delighted furrier. The couple left the shop with the girl drooling on the old man's arm. On Monday, the elderly gentleman appeared to find himself confronted by a furious shopkeeper. 'Your "niece" just came in to collect her coat, and she wasn't very pleased when I refused to hand it over because your cheque bounced. You're a scoundrel and a cheat,' he screamed. 'I know,' said the errant customer, smirking and proffering a bottle of Veuve Clicquot champagne. 'I'm sorry you had to go through that, but I've just come to apologise for the inconvenience and to offer my thanks for the most exciting weekend of my life.'

Only a joke, of course! And from many a young woman's point of view, it's a fine thing to be dated by a middle-aged man with the suave air and well-lined pockets that ageing affords so many of the male species. He is, for the most part, more sophisticated than a beer-swigging, slightly arrogant twenty-something. He knows how and where to wine and dine a lady with impressive panache. Even when he's broke, he will still somehow find the money to romance his new partner with the champagne, flowers and the expensive gifts he knows will impress her youthful naivety in the hope that the 'dolly-bird' adorning his arm will perform magic, reverse his own years, and turn him into a lothario in bed.

Scott, sixty-nine, has been searching for his perfect soulmate since his divorce twelve years ago. The Glaswegian former pharmacist admits he's looking for a woman aged between fifty and sixty. 'I wouldn't choose a woman of my own age,' he says. 'Anything between a nine and nineteen-year age gap would be perfect, although I wouldn't start a World War if the woman was even younger. A woman of sixty-nine might be past what I consider to be the most important part of married life, whereas men are never past anything.' Scott sees his ability to attract and woo younger women as a challenge. He admits, however, that although he frequently attracts a single date, he rarely manages to maintain a relationship beyond two meetings, and wonders why!

The reality – as seen by honest men

Actor and TV personality Jeremy Milne, forty-five and never married, says that after much trial and error, he has discovered he prefers dating women of his own era rather than women a generation younger. 'Recently, I have dated both women of my own age and younger women,' he says. 'I've discovered that women of my own age are so much more interesting to be with. It's the thing about life experience. What you have done;

your achievements; your highs, your lows, are all part of such a rich tapestry. These are the things that make both men and women attractive. I'm not sure whether there is a little social stigma attached to the fact that when we men reach middle age, we are supposed to be in the prime of life, steady and stable, but the myth is that when women reach the same age, they are grey-haired, wrinkled prunes well past their prime.'

Milne, one of the 'experts' to offer advice on communication skills to singles of all ages looking for love on the British TV programme *Would Like to Meet*, says: "When men or women reach mid-life and have apparently been unable to form a long-term or permanent relationship, they start to wonder how they have got into this situation. We question ourselves, 'How did this happen?' As soon as you start to think negatively like that, you begin giving off unattractive vibes about yourself. For whatever reason things have happened, they have happened. You need to turn the negatives into positives in order to move on. There is no point wasting emotional energy on 'what might have been if only . . .'

Milne suggests that men should generally think again about dating women in a different generation. When it comes to 'the age thing', he suggests:

- Searching out a point of common interest with a woman of your own age is far easier than searching for the same thing with a younger woman.
- You will find that the wealth of experience a woman of a similar age has gained through the years will make her a far more interesting and attractive companion than a woman twenty years her junior.
- The interests of a woman of your own age are far more likely to be in concert with your own.

Lying

Of course, you can lie about your age. Women can lose up to fifteen years from their chronological ages, just by keeping trim, and with the help of a few nicks and tucks in appropriate places, bottom lifts and HRT which can prolong their periods and strengthen their bones. Men, too, can resort to hair-dyes, hair implants and 'rugs' as well as plastic surgery. But it's not easy to keep up the pretence if you tend to forget that you ought not to be old enough to remember the Coronation or the excitement when England won the World Cup. Of course, you could always resort to the video or cinema as a good excuse for knowing what really happened, but by then it may be too late! Better to be (almost) honest than to get caught out in a big lie at the very beginning of a relationship.

Checklist for liars

If you do find yourself on a blind date with a man you suspect to be seventy when he's admitted to being only fifty-five – or, for that matter, a woman who admits she won't see fifty for another five years when you're convinced she's at least sixty-five, you might run through this light-hearted checklist for liars:

Checklist for her
1. Is he wearing a belt, braces or both? Belts indicate sixties style. He may be wearing braces because he has a hiatus hernia and belts are uncomfortable. Braces are 'in' among the under-fifties who wear suits. Belts and braces indicate the caution of age and experience. And he's taking no chances!
2. Designer labels, prominently splashed across the outside of his sweater/T-shirt. He's trying to prove how 'with-it' he is. Genuine younger middle-aged men will

---

go for the simple roll-neck and shirts will hang out below jumpers.

3. Does he wear Brylcreem instead of gel? If you're not sure, you could try the old trick of running your fingers through his hair – but watch out for a shock.

4. Before you try the above, look for clues that it isn't a toupee. Rugs don't usually match the colour of the hair around them particularly well and there may be a big 'ledge' at the back where they don't line up with natural hair. If you try the Brylcreem/gel test, you could end up with more in your hand than you bargained for.

5. Check his hands for age spots.

6. Drop something (anything) into the conversation about how you've heard that National Service, which was in force in Britain until the late-1950s, might cure the current problems with over-exuberant youth. If he's over sixty-five, he will be unable to restrain himself from boasting which of the armed services he served in or how he was excused.

7. Dance close-up. If you can't feel any energy, you may be dating a 'dead' loss.

If you've ticked more than two of the above, you may do well to challenge him chronologically before you get caught in a horizontal position which may prove deeply disappointing and from which it may be difficult to escape without a severe blow to your own ego. But don't be too critical, or he could turn the tables on you.

Checklist for him

1. Get loving. Get close and check her scalp line for signs of surgery. Does she have rather fuller kissing equipment than you might expect?

2. Does expression show on her face? If not, she's almost certainly a botox patient.

3. Is she wearing mini-skirts with support hose?
4. Insist you love the natural look – or suggest a date going swimming where all the make-up *has* to come off.
5. Does she have problems getting in and out of your sports car?
6. Does she ever complain about the 'time of the month'? Does she do it too often?
7. Does she suddenly go pink and start blushing heavily when you haven't said anything embarrassing and the room is freezing?
8. Does she always take KY jelly out of her bag when you get into the bedroom?

If you've both clearly been telling porkies, why not come clean and enjoy *all* the pleasures that maturity can bring to you in the relationship, in and out of bed.

Mistakes

It offers some solace, however, to know that men who swap their faithful, loving but often predictable wives for 'younger models' often realise their whopping mistake too late, and further down the line may seek out a woman of their own generation. When Rick Stein, who was in his mid-fifties, left his wife Jill for a much younger woman, he reportedly admitted to the British press that he knew he was going through a mid-life crisis. Apparently, he had said he was anguished in his fifties, rather than besotted with his new young woman. Once he'd started living with her, the newspapers claimed he lost interest and they reported that he'd told journalists how it was only after living with a very young woman that he realised he loves his wife after all. Unsurprisingly, reports insisted that she refused to take him back. As Linda Lee Potter wrote in the *Daily Mail* at the time:

'Clearly she no longer misses the presence of an ageing, self-obsessed chap, forever flossing his teeth, craving reassurance, flattery and attention, who no doubt did press-ups at dawn, constantly needed to be told he was looking good and flirted with pretty customers . . . other middle-aged men thinking of starting an affair would be wise to take note.'

Simon's experience

Simon, divorced in his mid-forties, admits that he rather fancied himself with a very young woman on his arm:

'After my marriage failed, I tried dating a couple of lovely women in their twenties,' he says. 'I felt a million dollars and twenty years younger with the first girl I dated. It was very flattering to find she found me sexually attractive. She seemed to hang on my every word. We sat down for a meal and started talking. That's when I realised it was a big mistake. She was interested in clubbing. Her knowledge of politics was zero. Indeed, she had little knowledge of, or interest in, world affairs, and she was into TV soaps big time. I had sons only a few years younger than this woman and I soon realised that her conversation was their conversation, not mine. I even suggested I might introduce her to one of them. By the end of the evening I was bored stiff mentally. I thought perhaps I'd just picked the wrong girl, so I tried again and a similar thing happened. I was completely uninterested by her and I could see she was only pretending an interest in me. It was a disaster. I realised that I needed a woman with whom I had an intellectual attraction as well as a physical chemistry, and I was far more likely to find that with a woman of around my own age. I am now with a woman five years my junior, and I wouldn't care if she were five years my senior: the joy is in our shared and common interests and humour.'

What are men scared of?

Are men frightened that older women will 'act menopausal' in the way in which perhaps their ex-wives may have done? Do they read too many magazine articles telling women how to beat the menopause and avoid 'dried prune-itis', and then decide that it isn't even worth testing beneath the skin of a slightly wrinkled but very experienced former plum? Or is it just that their egos need massaging?

Equally, how often does the younger woman stop to think about the consequences of dating a man fifteen, twenty, or even thirty years her senior? A young woman in her early thirties may be hugely flattered when an elegant late fifty-/early-sixty-something 'adopts' her, showers her with gifts and impresses his friends. Mostly, she hasn't thought beyond the large rock she hopes he'll place on her finger and the glamorous honeymoon he's promised if she agrees to wed. It may be that she is looking for the stability of a 'father-figure', but has she thought of the penalties she may incur in a decade or two hence when he may become sick and she becomes his full-time carer rather than his full-time wife?

The 'step' problem

As former Beatle Paul McCartney has discovered, marrying a (much) younger woman can cause all sorts of problems with offspring. McCartney was sixty when he married his second wife, Heather Mills. At thirty-four, she is only four years older than his daughter, Stella. The two women have reportedly found it hard to get on because Stella is said to resent her new young stepmother; a woman young enough to be her sister. Macca may feel well pleased with himself as he recaptures the passion of youthful existence with Heather. Heather, clearly bent on showing she is 'the perfect wife' has thrown herself into 'causes' espoused by his late first wife, Linda. McCartney may see it as a second bite at the cherry. But in ten years' time, will the former Beatle be quite so enthralled by his brides' enthusiasm? Will he not wish he'd settled for a quieter and less frantic existence while she is still eager to get out there and show the world what she's made of? When he becomes a grandparent, can he expect her to fulfil the role of 'Grandma'? Heather Mills McCartney has already let it be known that she's keen to start a family of her own. Could she embrace mother-hood and step-grandmotherhood at one and the same time? Would the rivalry between stepmother and stepdaughter extend a generation to half-brother/sister?

Children

A young woman may (quite naturally) want children of her own. As men do remain fertile well into old age (witness Charlie Chaplin whose youngest was born when he was well over eighty), it's perfectly possible. McCartney may yet be intent in fulfilling his young wife's hopes for children of her own. Luckily, he too is in a position to be a distant, adoring, rather than hands-on, dad. But without the financial wherewithal to retain a team of nannies and childcare support staff, when push comes to shove, will an ordinary mature husband who has done it all before really relish being woken at three in the morning by a colicky screaming baby?

'Women accept what they are and they are comfortable with who they are and what they have become,' says Linda Davis, Chairperson of the Association of British Introduction Agencies (ABIA). 'A man with a beer paunch and a bald head, let loose for the first time in decades, may mentally believe himself to be the same, handsome, sexually appealing and suave guy he was the last time he was single in his twenties or thirties, when in actual fact the physical truth is quite different. However, all men are Peter Pan at heart.'

Can the odds be beaten?

Even allowing for the facts and figures, can a determined woman beat 'the age thing' that seems somehow fixated in the male psyche? I think she can. Of course, none of us can produce a host of handsome Pearce Brosnan or Roger Moore look-alikes to order. Redressing the balance is more than any one person could hope to achieve in a lifetime, let alone a single book. Certainly, there is no magic formula to fix the chemistry between two individuals of any age or status. However, I firmly believe that you can meet a man or woman in your own peer group *if you really want to make it happen*. Earlier in this chapter, I have played devil's advocate, explaining the rationale behind the apparent divergence of figures, but it really is not *all* doom and gloom: you *can* meet a man in your age group, and you *can* find a compatible and loving partner. However, *you* are the person who has to make it happen. There's no point sitting at home, bemoaning your fate and waiting for the right man to drop from heaven into your lap. If you want a partner, you have to go out and actively look for one. That doesn't mean turning into a 'man-hunter'. One facet of dating that doesn't change, no matter whether you are young or old, male or female, is that if you appear too keen, act as though you are desperate or become too obsessive, you will frighten any decent man or woman away. The wider you broaden your friendship/acquaintanceship circle, the more you raise your chances of meeting a new and exciting partner – a person in an age-group you find acceptable and one with whom you can share interests, experiences and possibly a future.

Older woman; younger man

When a woman is in her forties, fifties, or even sixties, and should she dare to suggest meeting up with a younger man, she will almost certainly be accused of looking for a 'toy boy'

– unless, that is, her name is Joan Collins. No one can fully explain why one is perfectly socially acceptable and the converse totally unacceptable. If an older man hooks a younger woman, it's all a case of 'nudge-nudge, wink-wink' and 'clever devil', but when a woman announces her intended commitment to the younger man at her side, the world prejudges her as a 'silly old fool', and, in the case of a celebrity such as Joan Collins or Zsa Zsa Gabor, will add an insult such as: 'Can't she see he's after her money?' or 'Who does she think she's kidding?'

Some converse age-gap relationships do happen, and can work very successfully. Yet it is still a brave middle-aged, second-time-around man who dares admit he's hit the jackpot dating and marrying an older woman. As they get older, women may no longer want or be able to bear children. This doesn't mean they've become old crones with dried-up bodies and no sexuality at all: they are often vibrant, attractive, voluptuous women who, freed from fears of reproduction, have become more alluring and sexier than ever. What's more, they won't be bothering their 'toy boys' by constant reference to the loud ticking of their biological clocks. Older women are ready, willing and able to devote their time instead to enjoy completely carefree dating. They make great companions and experienced sexual partners, more so because they're not dominated by the thought of babies or the fear of producing unwanted offspring. Chances are, an older woman has children old enough to fend for themselves. The most pressing subject on her mind is building a warm, exciting relationship and having fun with the younger man who can truly appreciate *all* her assets.

Two who proved it could be done

Barbara and Russell

Barbara is forty-eight, and is a professional fund-raiser who loves dancing. She joined a country and western club in order to indulge her passion for keeping those feet tapping but without the need for a regular partner. When Russell, thirty-four, invited her to dance, she was delighted:

> 'We danced together several times during one particular evening and got on very well. It felt as though we were meant to be together, even that early on. I mentioned I had been line dancing and he said that was something he'd like to try, so I suggested he came to a class with me the following weekend. I realised he was a lot younger than me, so thought it only fair to tell him how old I was on our third date. I asked him how old he was, and then made my admission. I wanted it aired sooner rather than later in case he was uncomfortable with the idea of dating an older woman. I didn't want it to become an issue. When he told me he didn't mind a bit, I felt wonderful. The relationship is still very new and I don't know whether it will last. For a start, I'm not sure if he wants a family. I don't have any children and it's too late for me to start a family now; I think it's too soon to discuss that issue yet. But we get on so well that it is clear that we have something very strong between us and we are meant to be together. My friends are mostly envious. They say: "Lucky old you!" '

Pat and Andy

Andy was thirty-eight when he first met Pat, who was then fifty-five, and a four-times married mother of eight (including two foster children). They bumped into one another at an over-forties singles social near her Staffordshire home. They married a couple of years ago after a long courtship and although Andy admits he was looking for a younger woman by whom he could father a family of his own, he says that after two years of marriage, he wouldn't swap Pat for a younger model for all the world:

'I had just come out of a four-year-long relationship with a woman thirteen years younger than myself at the time Pat and I first met. We had even got engaged, but the relationship just fizzled out. I think we ran out of conversation. I went along to the over-forties night because what's a year or two here or there. Before the four-year relationship, I'd been going out with a woman six years older than me. When Pat and I first met and she told me she had eight children, six of her own and two foster children, and that she'd been married four times, I was sure she was *not* the one for me. What attracted me most, though, despite her family and all those marriages, was her personality. There was something about her I couldn't help liking. She was so lively and bubbly. More bubbly, and with a younger outlook, than many women half her age. Pat is certainly not the norm. Then we discovered we had other interests in common. Both of us are spiritualists. She had been going to the Spiritualist Church for about five years. I had been going for more than twenty-four years. I used to go with my mum and dad. When she told me about her life experiences, I realised that she had a huge experience of life and not all of it was happy, yet she managed to shrug it off in a way a younger woman might find hard. She just accepts it and gets on with it. She is a very independent lady and I like sharing my life with someone who's happy for our relationship to be a proper partnership all the way round. Not that we don't have our arguments. Of course we do. Especially now we're running a hotel together. She tells me what to do, and I do it! When we first got together, Pat knew I wanted children and investigated the idea of egg donation and IVF for me. I admired her tremendously for that. We were turned down by several clinics on the grounds that Pat was too old and I have resigned myself to not having children of my own now. Although hers are grown-up, I get on brilliantly with her sons. Her oldest son and I are only a couple of years apart and we go to play pool together at least once a week. They are my family too now. I do love Pat, and despite the jesting, I wouldn't swap my older wife for a younger model for anything.'

2

What am I looking for?

If you're reading this book, you are obviously keen to find love mid-life. But what do you want? And are you ready for it?

Every woman (and, I suspect, every man) who finds herself single mid-life has experienced rejection by a partner at one time or another. As a result, some are looking for clones of the partner they've lost. Others think they want a complete opposite. Ideas become set in stone. You may find a partner, but you won't find love if you're not ready for it.

Am I ready to find love again?

Ask yourself:

1. Am I really missing out by losing my former partner?
   Yes ❑   No ❑
2. Is he/she really worth the anguish I'm feeling?
   Yes ❑   No ❑
3. Was there really any hope of retrieving the relationship, and was it worth it anyway, when my former partner was so ready to abandon it? Yes ❑   No ❑

4. Is what I feel for my former partner really love?
    Yes ❏   No ❏
5. Am I better off without them? Yes ❏   No ❏

If you have answered more than three of the above five questions positively, you *are* ready to put your life back together and move forward. The trick is to recognise that a former partner can't hurt you any more. Whatever you once had together is over. But the second, and in my opinion most important, lesson you have to learn is to take your new search for love at a steady pace.

Don't rush out and plunge into a relationship with the first person who comes on to the scene just because having someone at your side is better than being alone. It's not. Finding yourself a new partner and talking yourself into a state of 'being in love' for the sake of it is generally a recipe for disaster.

Love changes

Love is different when you're older. And the kind of love you feel for one person may be totally different from the kind of love you feel for another. Of course, you still want the world to light up when the object of your affections enters the room, you still want to wait with anticipation for the phone to ring, but age and experience have taught you that the phone won't always ring when you want it to. The people you meet don't always match up to expectations, and when they don't, you need to find pleasure in other things.

Desperation for a relationship has a 'smell' about it and it's not an attractive aroma. When you reach mid-life, love *is* attainable. It *is* desirable. It *can* be as lovely and as wonderful as the first time round, if not even sweeter. However, it is no longer all-consuming. You have a lifetime of experience behind you. One of the most vital lessons of all when you go seeking love mid-life is learning how to bide your time.

Be realistic

Ask a room full of singles of both sexes what they think they want in a partner and you'll discover that the answers are woolly, mostly unrealistic and thus unattainable. 'I'd like to find a nice man,' Mary, fifty-one, told me. 'Nice' being a common adjective used by partner-hunters of both sexes. The former wife of a store manager, Mary had very definite ideas about the career of her yet-to-be-met spouse. 'I'd like to meet a professional man – a doctor or solicitor, someone well-heeled,' she told me. 'He must be kind, have a good sense of humour, and enjoy theatre and eating out. I'd prefer a man taller than me (she's 5'6"), older than me by about five years. I'd like him to be slim and fit, although not a gym junkie, and I hope he'd enjoy Chinese food, which is my particular favourite. I'd like it if he had children of similar ages to mine. I don't want to do the "kiddy thing" again. But I don't think I'm ready for step-grandchildren, yet. I'm not sure if I want a permanent relationship. It would just be good to have a man to take me out – no strings.'

The parameters of Mary's 'wish list' are improbable, if not impossible to fulfil. When I asked her whether she was prepared to compromise on any of them, she wavered very slightly. 'Well, maybe a little. But I'm not prepared to accept "anything in trousers".'

I then described a potential date to Mary. Someone had asked me whether I knew anyone who might like to meet a good-looking dentist of her own age. 'He's only 5'7", so you'd be taller than him if you were wearing heels,' I told her. She agreed to concede on height. 'He's got two married daughters and one small granddaughter – and I think he prefers cinema to theatre. But you almost fit his "wish list" because he's a South African immigrant and is desperate to meet a woman who owns her own house.' His expectations were, of course, as unrealistic as hers. I often wonder what might have happened had I put them in a room together without saying a word.

False starts

We all have false starts. Each new relationship is filled with possibilities. They won't all become probabilities and it's easy to feel disheartened when it all goes pear-shaped. But as a divorced friend said to me recently: 'After you've been through a marriage or relationship that didn't work, a bad date isn't that big a deal.' What's important is *not* to view every new person you meet instantly as a possible partner for life.

You may be physically attracted, only to discover that when the chemistry wanes, you are bored. You may find that what you initially believe to be a meeting of minds may not be the fitting jigsaw you thought it might be at first. You may go on a date for nothing more than just a pleasant evening's entertainment and find, as I did, that love can grow gradually and sweetly when you are in your forties and fifties in a way that wasn't in your emotional vocabulary when you were younger. You may be convinced after one or two meetings that you have finally found the love you've been looking for, only to become rapidly bored because you don't want what you thought you wanted most.

My first dating experience was with a man who showered me with chocolates and bouquets of flowers which appeared at the front door almost daily. This man would always come bearing expensive gifts. At first, it felt wonderful. No man had treated me this way in years and I thought I loved it. But then I ran out of vases and the whole thing became boring. When there's no fun in the relationship, stop it before you get in too deep and you both feel hurt and despondent.

Friendship or true love? Your attitude

Do you know what you want? Is it comradeship or a true love affair? If you date a new potential partner, do you read too far ahead into the possible relationship?

- Will I be content if this person and I date with no strings attached?
- Is this first date with this person the beginning of a deep and meaningful liaison?
- Could this new date become my lifetime partner?

If you can honestly answer the first question with a 'yes' and believe the other two to be outrageous at this stage, then you have the right attitude. Expect nothing and you may be surprised. Expect too much and you will be haunted by disappointment that in turn leads to feelings of rejection. You may be pushing yourself backwards instead of taking up the reins and galloping ahead.

Know yourself

When you embark on dating in mid-life, accept that you're not going out to 'buy' a new partner off a shelf in a store. (They come in several sizes and colours, Madam, but I'm not sure we've actually got one to fit you in royal blue . . .)

If you start off with a fixed and inflexible idea of a future partner, and only someone conforming to your pattern of looks, presentation, likes, dislikes and financial status will do, then you could be in for a very long partner-trawl.

Before you can hope to find the sort of partner you want, you need to know more about yourself. Take a sheet of paper and draw a line down the middle of the page. Head the left-hand column 'Things I Like about Me'. Head the right-hand column 'Things I Don't Like About Myself'.

The left-hand column should be longer than the right-hand one. Can you change anything in the right-hand column? This is for your eyes only, so be honest. However, it doesn't mean that you should put yourself down either. Your right-hand column might simply be revealing a lack of self-confidence and self-esteem. There are many courses you can take to build self-esteem and it might be well worth investing in one such course. *There is no point in expecting your date to think you are wonderful if the only person who doesn't believe it is you yourself.*

Make a list of the things you consider as most important to your everyday contentment.

- Do you eat to live, or live to eat?
- How importantly do you rate books in your life? What kind of books do you enjoy reading?
- What newspapers do you read?
- Do you enjoy music, and if so, what kind?
- Are you more entertained by theatre, cinema or TV?
- Do you love travelling, and if so where? Where did you spend your last holiday?
- Do you like dancing?
- Do you enjoy physical exercise?
- Are you house-proud? How important is it to you to live in a tidy and neat home?
- How importantly do you rate looks in a future partner?

Now draw up a *realistic* partnership 'wish list':

- What is the most important characteristic in a new partner?
- What are your pet hates in people of the opposite sex?
- Is hair colour (or looks) vital to your choice?
- What interests would you hope to share?
- Is the financial status of a future partner of prime importance?

If you are one of those happy souls who lives to eat and your frame reflects your pleasure, there's little point in thinking you'd be able to settle happily with a beanpole partner who eats to live. If you insist that you'd prefer a partner with blond hair rather than brown, you're omitting half the population at a stroke. If you love sun and warmth, would you be happy to share leisure with a partner whose idea of bliss is Iceland in winter?

Don't prejudge the contents entirely by the packaging. Rather concentrate on likes and dislikes. If you're a political animal, it can be fun to discuss and debate a political issue, even if you hold diverse opinions. But it would be no fun at all to be committed to someone who is entirely uninterested in politics and prefers discussing the feeding habits of their pet Alsatian dog. On the other hand, you could find yourself entirely fascinated by the feeding habits of Alsatians, and your new date could be equally as intrigued by your political knowledge. You'll never know until you try.

Pretend you are writing an advert for your dream partner for a lonely hearts column. What would attract you? What would turn you off? Where could you compromise?

Looks

Psychologists say that we judge the people we meet by the way they look within sixty seconds of that first crucial meeting. So, if you're very particular about the way you dress, you won't be too impressed by the man who dates you dressed in an old anorak and trainers. And if a well-dressed, cool-looking guy, who has taken the trouble to 'Grecian 2000' his hair, is greeted on a first date by a salt-and-pepper ex-'flower-power' lady with her hair in a bun, wearing a shapeless shift down to her ankles and a vast pashmina over it, he is unlikely to be bowled over, even if the pair do share a passion for butterflies.

Whether you will share empathy and chemistry as well as interests and tastes may well depend upon first impressions. You will judge dates by first appearances – and that's when people will make first impressions of you. To start with, question your own feelings about the initial impact you will make on any stranger.

- Do you consider yourself 'smart'?
- Are you happy with your weight?
- Do clothes concern you – or are you perfectly content to slob out in your old jeans?
- Are you particular about keeping your nails neat or manicured and your shoes polished, or are such things immaterial to your way of life?
- Are you a regular visitor to the hairdresser or do you care for your hair your own way?

Intellect

If you don't have a meeting of minds and plenty to talk about almost instantaneously, you may as well forget it. There is nothing worse than spending any length of time with someone you can't have a conversation with. Pregnant pauses give birth to hostility. Nevertheless, it may be as well to ask yourself how much importance you place on and how much your natural conversation is dominated by:

- family;
- food and drink;
- politics and world affairs;
- books, reading, theatre and cinema;
- dancing;
- hobbies such as bridge, Scrabble, pub quizzes, or physical activities such as walking, skiing, swimming or mountaineering.

You must have a point of mutual contact to open conversations. Conversation about *Coronation Street* characters or how you would react if one of the cast of *Friends* or *Home and Away* were your son or daughter could be very limiting. There's little point embarking on a relationship, whether for companionship, love or more, if you can't squeeze two words on a subject of common interest out of your potential partner. If you are naturally a physical person who loves walking, riding and outdoor pursuits, there's little point in long-term dating a couch potato whose principal interest is TV soap operas.

Be flexible

If you're hunting for a lifetime partner, you MUST be flexible. Be prepared to date people who may not appear immediately appealing 'on paper'. However, I must say that I disagree with the professional matchmaker who recently told me that many middle-aged women are, in her opinion, 'too fussy'. When you reach a certain time of life, there are some traits and characteristics in someone else which you will not put up with – and that is not unreasonable. I think being 'fussy' is preferable to taking a partner for the sake of it. More so at a time when one in three of all marriages ends in divorce, and the ratio is higher still for those who marry late or second time around. Only ever do what you are comfortable with.

Being 'fussy' is a positive, in my opinion. After all, why should you lower your standards? Being 'picky' is something else. Don't fix a profile of the person you want to meet and refuse any date with anyone who doesn't fill your expectations down to the last detail. If we all did that, no one would meet anyone! Even if you do find perfection, the odds are that the perfect person won't think you're perfect – so you'll be back to square one. Set standards, of course, but broaden horizons. A woman recently wrote to me saying she wanted to meet a graduate in his sixties and asked me where all the over-sixty graduates went to ground. I wrote back and asked her why she insisted on a graduate. There are many highly intelligent gentlemen in their sixties who never had the opportunity to go to university because of having to do National Service. However, many *are* successful businessmen. I pointed out places where she might go to meet intelligent people of both sexes, such as the University of the Third Age (U3A), which has branches all over the British Isles, and if she were mixing with intelligent people, then surely their friends would be intelligent too. She wrote back a delightful letter saying that she'd just been to her first U3A meeting, had loved every second of it, and although she hadn't yet met the partner she hoped to find, she thought she was going to love studying psychology; something she'd wanted to do for many years.

Finance

You may believe that money can't buy love. Of course it can't. It can't buy happiness either, but, as my late mother used to say, it's easier to be miserable in comfort! However, if it's money you're seeking as a prime consideration in a new partnership, you can't expect to find love too, and I think you're reading the wrong book! Although finance is important in the final analysis (more of this in the final chapter on how to make a partnership work), don't make it a priority on your dating wish list.

Maureen's expensive experience

When Maureen's colleague suggested she might like to meet a friend of her brother's, she agreed readily. He sounded so perfect. They chatted on the phone on several occasions and then agreed to meet for a meal. When they met, she was pleasantly surprised. He was well-groomed and excellent company, and his conversation suggested he was well-heeled. At the end of the evening, he insisted he would pay the bill, despite her protestations that it might be a good idea to go halves. He fumbled first in one pocket, then in another, blushed appropriately, apologised profusely, and explained that he'd obviously left his wallet at home. 'I paid up and he told me that of course, it would be his treat next time,' she says. 'We arranged to meet a couple of evenings later to go to the cinema. We arrived and he blushed again and told me that he hadn't been paid and didn't have any cash but didn't want to cancel our rendezvous.' Maureen believed him. She invited him home and he looked very glum. He spun her a hard luck tale about how things were financially difficult, but that once a large some of money he was owed was paid, he'd be fine.

'Call me gullible, but I believed him. I was so lonely, I think I'd have believed a man who attached wings to his back and called himself an angel. It was the first time someone had been really kind and apparently thoughtful towards me in years. He kept assuring me that he would have the cash "soon". I didn't even catch on when he asked me how much I earned. Idiot that I was, I actually told him. He told me I was wonderful. Beautiful. Clever. He loved me. I yearned to hear those words. They cost me dear. Of course, "soon" never did come and by the time I'd realised I was being dated by a money-grabbing skunk who cared for the look of my flat, the size of my car and the depth of my purse far more than he cared about me as a person, I had spent several hundred pounds on our dates, and it was money I could ill afford.'

Social status

I may be hounded for daring to voice this politically incorrect view, but I believe that the class system is alive and well and living in the UK, as well as in most other democracies. For the most part, neither men nor women want to find their standards of living compromised downwards by a new partner from a different background, with entirely different standards to those with which they are familiar. If home is a six-bedroom, four-bathroom country mansion with live-in help to attend to your every domestic chore or need, could you really adjust to life cooking vegetable pie in his two-bedroom council house on a large estate? Equally, you may find it hard to prepare dinner parties for (or have conversation with) a chamber full of judges, or a consultancy practice full of medics if you work as a shop assistant. That is not to say there will always be disharmony in a relationship between a shop assistant and a judge, but conversation and common interests may be somewhat limited, and without common points of reference, any relationship is doomed.

Before I'm bombarded with protests, I have to admit there will always be exceptions to any such generalisations. For example, the unlikely marriage of convicted armed robber John McVicar, sixty-six, and his new wife, the forty-four-year-old Countess Valentina Artsrunik, the woman he met when she edited his biography, seems to be working out a couple of years down the line. It must be said that they do both have crime in common! The unconventional countess is known for her penchant for former convicts. She was once engaged to convicted murderer Dorian Lester, and she herself spent five months in prison in Virginia before being found not guilty of shooting the jeweller George Moody in 1997.

The 'in common' factor

You need an 'in common factor' for many reasons:

- By the time you reach middle age, you probably have a family, including children who have been raised with certain standards that they take for granted. Changing life-standards in mid-life is hard, if not impossible.
- You are surrounded by friends you treasure. These people in your circle you love dearly. They may have stood by you through thick and thin. It is easy to be flexible financially and physically when you are a young couple building a life

together. Friendships you form in early life may fall by the wayside. It's harder to lose friendships as a result of an entirely changing lifestyle when you are older, especially given all the other hurdles you may need to overcome.

Sex? Is it now or never?

You are alone. You are celibate. You may have been involuntarily celibate for months or years. So when you go looking for love, is it sex you are after, and if so, how much and how soon?

Ask yourself:

- Am I looking for pure sexual activity, love, or a mixture of both?
- What were my views on dating and sex when I was a single teenager?
- Will a man think I'm 'easy' if I jump into bed with him on the first or second date?
- Do I need to take precautions if I'm no longer fertile?
- Will making him/her 'wait' gain me brownie points?
- Can I separate pure sex from love?

The last question is by no means the least important. I believe that the need to feed our sexual beings can be as important to good health as the need to eat nutritiously, and this applies in mid-life as potently as it applies when we are young. However, you can't starve yourself for months and then, when you're suffering from malnutrition, stuff yourself with sweet, rich food to make up for the deprivation, only to return suddenly to starvation rations again and expect to stay healthy. You'd not only upset the balance of your stomach, but your brain could end up playing tricks on you, and you would almost surely end up physically sick and more severely malnourished than before.

Believe it or not, the same is true of sex. I think that if you overdo the sex side of things with a new partner immediately, you may discover that although you've fulfilled a physical need, the emotional attachment you yearn for isn't there, and you can end up feeling twice as empty as you did before you embarked on a short, sharp sexual affair. There's no doubt that some women can, and do, find sex without love satisfying. Personally, I have found that no matter how sexually hungry I have ever been, I need an emotional as well as a physical attachment to satisfy my appetite. After speaking to many other single, mid-life women, I believe that the same applies to the majority of those of us looking for love and long-term commitment. It's very downhearting to go on a date with someone who soon makes it clear that what they're actually after is your body, and not you as a person.

If sex is all you're looking for, be wary. The man or woman who's ready to jump into bed with you on a first date may claim it's overwhelming chemistry that is forcing the issue but you can bet your bottom dollar that if they're willing to do it with you, without getting to know you just a little better, then they've been equally willing to do it with someone else. As a medical friend of mine once told me: 'An erect penis has no conscience.'

I'll never forget the man who announced at the end of our second date, a lunchtime shopping trip, that he had something special to show me. He produced a piece of paper and I studied it in horror. It was the result of an AIDS test, done between our first date and what was about to prove our last. 'I had it done specially for you,' he said proudly. He expected sex with me. He expected it, I think, in return for dating me. That's not the way I behave and, I have to say, he went out of the door rather more quickly than he came in it!

Everyone has his or her own sexual standards. Whether you decide to jump into bed with a stranger on a first date, or you wait to see whether the relationship includes more permanent promises, or you are of the opinion that you shouldn't go to bed until you are married, the choice is yours. By mid-life, we all have our personal standards of sexual behaviour. There is no general right or wrong.

Don't permit yourself to be pressured into a sexual relationship you don't want or aren't ready for because you feel you may 'lose' your new partner if you don't go along with their persuasive arguments (the favourite is, of course, 'Well, you aren't going to get pregnant now, are you?').

Remember

HIV and herpes are virulent infections spread by intimate sexual contact. They are on the increase, and they know no age boundaries. Syphillis and gonorrhoea, chlamydia and non-specific urethritis, although treatable, are as prevalent as ever. Genital warts are hard to treat and are spread by sexual contact. The temptation not to use protection is enormous when pregnancy is no longer threatened. Using condoms for protection against the spread of disease is the sensible option, and certainly until you have been in the relationship for long enough to know that you are not with an infected partner. Few people are virgins in mid-life. Few singles will *not* have had sex with at least one other partner – and who knows how many people that partner has had sex with?

Give every date a chance

You may not initially 'fancy' a first date, but if you get on, be prepared to give *every* date a chance of blossoming into friendship.

If you go on a first date and get on well enough, even if you're not blown away with emotion, why not give it a second and even a third chance: just as you won't discover all the worst points of someone at a first or second meeting, you won't discover all their best and most attractive points, either. *If you give yourself the luxury of time to work at and achieve a firm friendship and to appreciate one another's best qualities, emotional attachment can follow naturally.* Of course, there are people who claim they've fallen in love at first sight in mid-life. It's rare. Experience has shown me that time is the most crucial factor for mature people who hope to form lasting relationships.

Give a relationship time to develop and:

- You may be surprised at how you may uncover the most enticing traits in someone who was not instantly appealing.
- Be ready to let a relationship run a while before you insist that it can't go anywhere, unless, that is, you find your new date totally abhorrent.
- You may find it fun learning to like someone. Learning to be friends is the first step towards falling in love in mid-life. You may be lucky enough to find fireworks on a first date – but fireworks do have a habit of exploding in glorious technicolour and then fading to dull grey ash. Real, worthwhile relationships take time to grow.
- You may find your new partner displays appealing characteristics you've never thought of. But do be realistic. I know I've said it before, but I can't say it often enough.

Forget 'in the image of'

Never insist that a future partner must be a clone of a former partner. Despite all the recent amazing scientific claims, I don't believe they can clone partners, yet.

Divorcees or widowed people are as prone to pick former partner look-alike-act-alikes as anyone else. Many of those who've never married seek out cardboard cut-outs of the person with whom they had their most enduring and emotional relationship. It's very common for women who've been battered to embark on new relationships with men who eventually batter them. And the same goes for those people who marry alcoholics. Often, women in particular suffer because they come to see themselves as deserving such brutal behaviour. They believe that they have no choice but to accept it. If you've been the recipient of cruelty in any way, shape or form, you don't have to accept it again. *You don't deserve it. You're worth far more. You just need to believe in yourself.*

You CAN do it:

- Be prepared to try new experiences. If the date doesn't work, all you've lost is one evening.
- Open your mind to new ideas and experiences which you may find equally as enticing, exciting and irresistible as old ones – and do let go of 'what was'.
- Be prepared to widen your experiences by dating people you might have thought unsuitable in the past.

Value yourself NOW

Value yourself for what you are NOW rather than for what you were twenty years ago. Ask yourself: Would I really like to be twenty again?

- Don't waste time and energy grieving for the person you were in the past.
- Don't think about the relationships you may have had that have failed.
- Forget about the changes that have taken place in the way you look, the way you think or your lifestyle.
- Concentrate on the way you are now and on making the most of yourself.

If you try to be someone other than yourself on a date in order to impress, you will be tense and you will end up making a terrible impression. In the end, the truth will out.

What sort of date might make you happy?

Dr Sidney Jones, a lecturer in psychology at London University who specialises in mid-life relationships, believes that if you want to be liked – and indeed loved – by other people, then first you need to like yourself. If you have self-esteem, then your personality instantly becomes attractive. And in order to date successfully, you also need to have a positive attitude towards your efforts at inventing a new life for yourself. Relying on other people to build your life for you is just not enough, although there's nothing wrong with accepting help along the way.

When it comes to seeking a partner in later life, Dr Jones points out, 'shopping' for a new partner can't be compared to buying an electric toaster. When you buy the toaster, you know that you not only want an electrical gadget that will brown your bread, but you want it in a colour or material, aluminium or otherwise, to match the other gadgets in your kitchen. You have a list of 'positives' that need fulfilling. When you go seeking a potential life partner, however, you need to give yourself permission to look at the options.

'What you are looking at is a potential relationship, and you find out who you are from the way in which you react to potential partners. Some people never discover who they really are, because they are measuring themselves according to someone else's judgement of them. It's what is known in psychological academia as the "looking glass self". We see ourselves as the way we are perceived by other people. That's not hypocritical or vain. It's just the way human beings are.'

Certainly, anyone who has ever been married or been in a long-term relationship and who is planning to start dating again needs to be sure that loneliness doesn't overwhelm their judgement. Many mature people find the spectre of loneliness grows ever more daunting as the years pass and date anyone of the opposite sex, no matter how unsuitable, because they think they might prove a possible means of assuaging the misery of loneliness. They panic. 'This has to be it,' they say to themselves. 'I'm running out of time.' And then, when they're in so deep that extricating themselves from the web of the relationship is no longer a matter of just saying 'goodbye', they find they're caught up with a man or woman who is causing them far more problems than they solve.

The manipulator

Jill, a forty-eight-year-old divorcee, found herself in a dilemma because, she admits, she fell into the trap of going for outer looks and accepting similar behaviour patterns from a new date. All twenty-six years of her marriage, her husband had manipulated her. She was constantly emotionally blackmailed to go wherever he wanted to go, to do whatever he wanted to do, and to behave how he expected her to behave without question.

When an apparently charming man, introduced to her by friends, invited her out, she was flattered and delighted to accept.

'I admit he bore a slight resemblance to my first husband in build and colouring. We enjoyed a lovely meal in a local restaurant and I did quite fancy him. Warning bells began to sound as he ordered the meal, asking me only what I didn't like, rather than what I did and then ordering for me. He chose the wine without asking whether I preferred red or white and as the meal progressed, and we talked, further niggling doubts arose, yet I felt I was becoming paranoid and that not every man I went out with would be like Paul, my ex. I thought I really ought to give this seemingly pleasant guy a chance. When, as dessert was being served, he asked if I was prepared to share an adventure, I hadn't worked it all out and said it might be fun, depending on what it was. He took some tickets from his pocket and waved them at me triumphantly. "I've booked for us to go across the Channel early on Saturday morning. I'll pick you up at 5 a.m. We'll drive down to Dover, catch a hovercraft across to Boulogne and have breakfast. Then I've ordered a car and we'll toddle around, have lunch, go to the hypermarket and come back on *Sea Cat*."

'I thought him somewhat presumptuous to have arranged the whole thing without discussing it with me first, but it was the sort of thing my ex might have done. Perhaps, I thought, I was wrong about men all the time. Perhaps this is what all men do. Paul was forever making plans for us without asking me first. Perhaps we might have been compatible after all and I'd just kicked up too much of a fuss? At this stage, I had forgotten all the awful things I'd been forced to do within the marriage against my will. Wasn't this "organisation" just what I had been missing?

'When my date turned up in faded jeans, wearing a heavy gold necklace and driving gloves with holes in the knuckles, I knew this was not a carbon copy of Paul. Paul would never have worn driving gloves, for a start! I tried to have a conversation of the kind Paul and I had once shared. I soon discovered he wasn't interested in my family. He knew nothing about politics and his world seemed to revolve around travel and food. Our conversation was stilted. I realised I was trying to recall a shared history I'd had with my former partner. Except the person I was trying to engage in this conversation was a complete stranger. At least, with Paul, there'd been chemistry at the outset.

'And it got worse. When we reached Le Touquet in the afternoon, he suggested a walk along the beach. We sat down on the sand and he started to kiss me and try more. Talk about an octopus. He had arms everywhere and the harder I tried to fight him off and tell him I didn't fancy him, the harder he tried to force himself. He was certainly "up for it".

Onlookers must have wondered about this middle-aged couple, fighting over a fumble on the beach. Eventually I won. It was a cool spring day and I was wearing so many layers, he couldn't find "me" underneath them! On the way back to Boulogne, we stopped for dinner, despite my protests. Over steak and frites, he told me we'd now been together for sixteen hours and then announced: "Although it's only the second time we've been out, that's the equivalent of at least five dates. If we're still together next week, we'll get married." I pointed out politely that I didn't want to marry him – and would he please be kind enough to get me home. It was one hellish journey! I had to keep the phone on answering mode to monitor his persistent calls for weeks afterwards. I wouldn't speak to him. Marry him, indeed! I suddenly realised that he was every bit as manipulative, probably more so, than my ex-husband. Now when I go on dates, I make sure that I only do the things I want to do. No man will ever manipulate me in any way, ever again.'

The expert view

Dr Jane Prince, Principal Lecturer in Psychology at the University of Glamorgan in Wales, who specialises in the study of life transitions, identity and ageing, says:

'There is a huge difference in dating behaviour between young people and those in middle age. It's all to do with the development of the self-schema – the clusters of knowledge you gather about yourself as you get older – and that includes your knowledge of yourself in relation to others as well as your own "possible selves". Possible selves are the range of outcomes that can result from taking or not taking a particular course of action. In a sense, your possible selves are both open to and constrained by past experiences as well as by expectations.

'For example, if in your youth you are brought up as one of a family of ten, and the most successful member or your family obtained two GCSEs at 'C' grade, you are unlikely to set your sights on making your fortune as a brain surgeon but, given TV programmes such as *Pop Idol*, you could quite realistically aspire to becoming a millionaire pop star. It's worth stating the positives and negatives plainly as a fair base-line from which to start the search for a partner.'

Ask most single women for a profile of their ideal man, and they will give you the same sort of description Mary gave me at the beginning of this chapter. Many women will insist they want to meet an 'educated man with a good sense of humour'. Understandable, of course. I used to say that too. But if you were once happily married to Bob the Builder, would you want to be the significant other of a professor of English second or third time round? If he was spouting Shakespeare or James Joyce round the dinner table, how would you cope? Equally, if your last long-term relationship was with a judge or a doctor, would you find yourself able to engage in riveting conversation with a refuse disposal operative (dustman, in old language)? You may think it desirable in your dreams to date an extrovert, but if you are quiet, shy and retiring, you could quickly become irritated and embarrassed by the presence of a constant court jester.

Dr Prince says:

'You place your own history and, to an extent, your social position will influence the possible selves you might have in the future. Life experiences play a major role not only in opening up but also closing down possible selves. As we get older, we all have more elaborate, "fear selves" of the person we don't want to become as well as the positive possible selves of who we want to be. That's why, the older you get, the fussier you get about the kind of person you want to spend your life with. But you may also be experiencing the fear self: "If I don't meet someone soon, I'm going to become a crotchety, lonely old man or woman." '

Dr Prince believes that there are enormous gender distinctions between the feared selves of men and women. She says:

- Women may not be as anxious to rush into a new relationship as men are, because on the whole they tend to have closer relationships with their children so they know that if they do have a family, whether they are divorced, widowed or single parents, they are unlikely to be without care or human contact in later life.
- Women find it far easier to confide in other women. Men rarely share confidences with other men.
- Women heterosexuals can accept the touch of another woman. Heterosexual men find it almost impossible to accept the touch of another man.
- Women tend to have more friendships than men do, although they are of shorter duration, but they will be of both sexes. Men have fewer close friends but their friendships often date back to teenage or student years.

Dr Prince adds: 'A girl-friend of mine was feeling very down after a relationship ended. I had a new, invigorating body scrub, and I offered to massage her with it as a tonic. A male friend of mine was horrified when he heard I had massaged her whole, naked body. He said no man would dream of doing such a thing but to us it came quite naturally, with no sexual overtones.'

Other people's perceptions

Dr Prince points out that in mid-life you no longer have the same kind of singles support network you had in earlier life. 'You have to point out that you are single, otherwise everyone automatically assumes you are in a long-term partnership, whether you wear a ring or not,' she says. It's a problem for both men and women. As long as you are hoping to go dating, a single same-sex best friend in a similar situation is essential. Not only because you have someone to physically go out with and to bolster one another's confidence, but because only someone who is experiencing what you are experiencing can really understand what's happening. And it is fun to share intimacies of the dating game with someone else who is doing it.

Forget about possible rivalries that may have dogged your younger years. Immature daters always want the partner someone else is dating because the grass is always greener on the other side. But, by mid-life, you will have a definite life-plan. It is unique to you. It's rare for two mature friends to be truly attracted to one man.

Avoid serial daters

While you are dating in a search for the love of your mid-life, it is well to know that there are a small band of 'serial daters' of both sexes out there, ready to set bait, entrap you, and then dump you with all the dignity of a crushed fly. Although in my experience, serial daters tend to be male rather than female, there are many women who love to talk about the string of men they've dated and then dumped in the past. If someone who has been single for ten, fifteen, even twenty years regales you with stories of their previous dates and then invites you out, beware!

'These people have no positive images of themselves as single people,' says Dr Prince. 'They can't find the woman of their dreams so they date one woman after another. They have no positive representation for being single and being male, whereas most women who want to be in a relationship have some positive past representation of themselves as singles.'

She suggests you ask yourself the following questions.
If I'm still single in two years' time:

- Where will I be?
- What will I be doing?
- Who will my friends be?
- If I break my leg and have to go into hospital, who will come and see me?

Now look at the other side of the coin. If I have a partner in two years' time:

- Where would I like to be?
- What would I like to be doing?
- Who will my friends be?
- Will the people who might have come to see me in hospital still come if I am with a partner?

Answering these questions as honestly as you can will show you how things can change. Change is always frightening. But as you mature, you know that everything does change. Your relationships have already changed if you are reading this book. Your parents change and need care – in effect, your role towards them changes and you become the 'parents' where they become the 'children'. Your children change and need an altogether different kind of support and care than you offered when they were small. Change is frightening, but you do need to think of it in a positive rather than a negative light. When people discuss ageing, they often think only of the negatives, of the loss of youth, the loss of opportunities, the loss of relationships. But throughout life there are positives too. What you are looking for in a new love in mid-life includes change – for the better.

3

Where to find a date

Meeting new singles was easy when we were in our teens and early twenties. Everyone was in the same boat. Most people were looking for partners – and there were plenty of places to go hunting. When we outgrew youth clubs, we could go clubbing or to pubs, bars, bowling alleys or coffee shops. We were often part of a crowd, which made group outings easy. The people you studied with or worked with were mostly singles too.

However, by the time you hit forty, most of your friends are in pairs. So when you find yourself newly single again, the reality that not everyone in your peer group is in the same situation can come as a bit of a shock. Yes, you've got plenty of friends, but they've got wives, husbands or long-standing partners. Wherever you go, you are the odd-bod, quite literally. If you go to a dinner party, more often than not, there is an odd number round the table and the odd one is you. Sometimes you've been 'set up' with a partner and, all too often, the 'friend-of-a-friend' is not someone you'd be seen dead with on a wet foggy Monday night in the Highlands.

Mature women suffer from another major disadvantage. Men of any age can sit comfortably alone in a pub, club or restaurant, waiting for the 'talent' to appear. But when you've grown up in a culture that teaches that 'nice' women don't sit sipping pints at the bar or go clubbing alone, it takes a brave lass or a foolhardy one, to try.

If there's an over forties night at a local pub or club, a single same-sex friend can be a valuable asset. When I first found myself alone, I remember someone advising me how important my single girl friends would be. If you can, though, go as part of a crowd rather than a twosome, otherwise you may find yourself in a sticky spot if one of you meets a potentially interesting date and the other doesn't – or if you both end up fancying the same person! Platonic opposite-sex friends can also be a great advantage, particularly if you're going clubbing or to a dance. They act as a buffer if you need it and you have the psychological security of being with someone else but the emotional freedom to meet and chat to whoever you please. *Remember, every new experience you try is also a new opportunity to meet someone of the opposite sex.*

Choose the right venues

One of my girl friends goes salsa dancing each week. She loves dancing but it's generally a difficult activity to pursue alone. But with salsa dancing, she doesn't need to go with a partner; she's met a number of single men who enjoy dancing and go along too, and she has had a number of dates as a result.

I used to go to a bridge class. Bridge is not the sociable game it's cracked up to be because if you're in a lesson, there's generally no time to chat except during the coffee break. Of course, many of the people who went to the classes I attended were married, but as a result of that class, I got invited to a number of social events where I made new single friends. And as soon as I was adept enough to sign in for supervised play, I met other people at my own level and we arranged games in one another's homes. If you join a general activity rather than a dedicated singles pursuit, it goes without saying that *not* everyone will be single. But you may be invited to other events as a result and you'll be surprised to discover just how many other singles there are out there in the same boat as you are.

Get out there

You will never find love mid-life if you sit at home waiting for the perfect man or woman to drop out of the sky. The dating wish-fairy doesn't work that way. You have to get on with your life, following the hobbies that interest you and taking pleasure from the entertainment you most enjoy or embarking on new avenues of interest. These are the places where you are most likely to meet a compatible partner, however unlikely that may seem. Don't say you've tried it and it doesn't work! Use a little imagination. If you always go to one particular bridge club for supervised play, do a little detective work and find another similar club in your area. If you always go to one gym and you already know everyone there, ask if your membership permits you to try another venue within the same group. Variety on a theme really is the spice of life. You may find that your interest group is going on a trip or outing to visit another group. Sign up and go along. It's sometimes hard to feel that you'll be welcome as a single. Take a deep breath, find the courage, and you could find the love of your life.

Count your advantages

As a mature single, appreciate your own qualities. Check out the following. Do you:

- Have more confidence in yourself than at any other time in your life (although a bad life-experience knock can dent your confidence badly)? Yes ❏   No ❏

- Have more money in your pocket than you had years ago?
  Yes ❑   No ❑
- Know exactly what you enjoy and what you hate?
  Yes ❑   No ❑
- Enjoy more freedom to pursue your interests in terms of time? Yes ❑   No ❑
- Know you don't have to do anything you don't want to, to please others? Yes ❑   No ❑

If you can tick 'yes' to at least three of the above, then finding a way of meeting new people should be relatively easy. At least you know that whatever you try, you are doing it because it's what *you* want to do. DON'T get trapped into going somewhere or doing something where you suspect you are unlikely to meet *your* kind of people. If you're an energetic type and your idea of fun is aerobics and line dancing, you're highly unlikely to find a compatible partner on an art appreciation weekend. If you don't drink, then the pub may be the wrong place to start seeking a new mate. If you're the intellectual type who loves classical music, you won't choose to spend an evening at a pop gig. And if you are forty-plus and would like to meet people of your own generation, there's no point in going to a youth club hop.

Some of the suggestions outlined in the following pages, of things you might try, may appear obvious, and I'm not trying to teach my grandmother (or grandfather) to suck eggs, but they may offer you a new slant on a tried and tested theme or an opportunity to explore something in a way you hadn't thought of. Don't dismiss any of them out of hand. Surprising things happen when you're least expecting them.

Aubrie and Jim

It may be that you're already going somewhere where you're entirely comfortable and that you have no thought of meeting a new partner. Indeed, it may be the last place you expect to meet a prospective mate. Then, fate takes a hand, just when you're least expecting it. Take my American friends, Aubrie and Jim.

Aubrie, fifty-five and a divorcee, and Jim, a sixty-year-old widower, were both members of the First Presbyterian Church in Tennessee in the USA. Both had belonged to different branches within the organisation for some five years. At the time they met, both had recently ended long-term relationships. Yet although they belonged to the same community, neither of them was aware of the existence of the other until they went on retreat into the mountains in July 2000. Aubrie says:

'Both of us love the mountains and nature and all that they encompass. There is a connection to the earth and to spirituality at the same time. Part of the retreat is to walk a labyrinth, a form of meditation, which is a series of pathways you follow. It is in the shape of a circle. You walk to the centre and then take the same path out again. That Saturday morning, we had had a speaker who came to talk to us about the Chartres Cathedral Labyrinth, and then I set out to walk the labyrinth alone. When you walk a labyrinth, you do so with intention: it was my intention to release a lot of my past. I was walking very meditatively, trying to free myself from my past, coming in touch with it and just letting it go. I had reached the centre, had made several turns and was just on my way out, as Jim reached the centre going inwards. We came face to face. We looked at one another. Time stood still for both of us. There were other people around, going in and coming out, but for us there was no one else there. It really was a very spiritual experience. We looked into one another's eyes and bowed to each other. At the same moment, we greeted one another with the East Indian greeting "*Namaste*". In the Indian language this means "I honour the divine within you". I had never done that with anyone else. Jim told me later that neither had he. Yet, at that moment, it was a natural occurrence for us both. I can't even describe the feeling that it triggered for both of us. It was a feeling of something bigger than we were individually; a connection between us. We stood there for perhaps ten seconds. It can't have been long because other people were walking the labyrinth and with just a single path, we were passing shoulder to shoulder. I went on out. He finished his walk and came on out. He told me later that he had been watching me from the sidelines all morning and had made up his mind that he wouldn't walk the labyrinth unless I did. At the time we met, neither of us was looking for love. Neither of us was expecting to find it. Yet both of us know we were guided to that point in time by something much larger and more powerful than either of us.'

The couple married in early 2002, and attend the same church still.

Disasters and how to overcome them

Select the wrong venues to seek out a mate, and you're likely to meet so many unsuitable people that you'll be tempted to give up, go home, and endure your lonely status quo. You may happen upon a group where you aren't comfortable, don't fit, and within which you may feel even more isolated than ever before. Or you may feel that you've entered a world filled with 'saddos', my acronym of sorts for what I call 'sad and desperate oddballs' – people who have no idea how to look after themselves properly, let alone treat a member of the opposite sex with the respect they deserve. I once met a woman at a lecture evening at a singles club and she invited me to tea on a Sunday afternoon. 'There are a group of us who are all single and meet for Sunday afternoon tea in other people's houses. Come along,' she invited. With nothing better to do, I accepted gratefully. She seemed a perfectly pleasant lady and I had nothing to lose.

It was only on arrival that I began to feel awkward. As I paid my £5 contribution on the door, I was asked to fill in a form. This was not just a form with the general name and address details one expects to be asked for the first time you go to any new singles event. It also asked for details of my work – and my income – which I decided to leave blank. I really couldn't see what business my income was to anyone I met over Sunday afternoon tea! Then I received the second shock of the afternoon. 'You will need to fill in the *whole* form before we can admit you,' I was informed sternly. 'Then you will be invited to attend a management meeting where the committee will assess your suitability to join us. We vet all our members carefully and we'll notify you if we think you're a suitable candidate to join.'

For one mad moment I thought I was at a job interview rather than a social event. Suitable candidate? Management committee interview? And I thought I was just going out for a cup of tea and some social chit-chat. Supposing they turned me down? I was mortified. And then angry. Who did these people think they were, inviting me to tea and then telling me that I needed to pass an interview to discover whether I was smart enough, rich enough, spoke in suitably clipped tones, and was socially acceptable enough to be invited to join their elite band? Perhaps I over-reacted when I told this jumped-up woman with a plum in her pseudo-aristocratic mouth that she could stuff their tea, their interview and their fiver. I thrust my shoulders back and marched myself out as haughtily as I could.

I got as far as the car door before I began sobbing. I felt socially and mentally inferior for no good reason. But I pulled myself together, threw the soggy tissues away and let logic overtake emotion. I'd stumbled into the wrong place at the wrong time and I'd learned never to go that route again. And it was very funny in retrospect. All these people, feeling so inferior themselves that they had to prove their superiority by lauding it over other vulnerable mortals. I started to laugh and couldn't stop giggling for hours, every time I thought of them trying to prove their social superiority like the television character Hyacinth Bucket (pronounced Bouquet) in the classic comedy series *Keeping Up Appearances*.

If you stumble upon a mishap, treat it as an 'experience'. *Don't let it put you off.*

The trick is perhaps to ask yourself a few pertinent questions before you embark on a new venture:

- Is this a social group where I am likely to meet other people with whom I will have something in common?
- Is there someone I can ask what it's all about before I venture along?
- Is this a hobby I'd really like to try although I've never had the opportunity to do it before?
- Am I likely to make *friends* of both sexes here?
- Why am I doing this?

Answer 'yes' to the first four questions and you're on the right track. Enjoy people, places and experiences for what they are. If you are lucky enough to meet someone special as a result, as Aubrie and Jim did, then look on that as a bonus. If you fall into the trap of finding yourself in the wrong place at the wrong time as I did, don't let it deter you for ever. Go along for the sake of making new *friends*. As I've said earlier in this book, new friends of both sexes can only be a bonus and who knows who they know?

BUT – If you find yourself somewhere you don't want to be, walk out. And don't let the experience daunt you. It's not you who is 'wrong'. It may not be them, either. Take it that you've accidentally landed up somewhere that's not right for you.

Some married friends once persuaded me to go to a singles dance. A male friend gave me a lift (no, really: he was *only* a friend). It took all the nerve I had to walk through the door, and as soon as I entered the room, I knew it was a ghastly mistake.

To my horror, the ladies' cloakroom was filled with a gaggle of middle-aged women slapping on the black eyeliner and the same white-pink Revlon Solitaire lipstick they had used in their teen dating days. They giggled in high-pitched voices as they powdered and painted, and discussed the 'talent' in the dance hall. The clock had miraculously turned back for them. This was dating the way they knew it, only now they were hiding their efforts at beautification and 'pull-dressing' not from disapproving parents, but from their own sons and daughters. Their faces 'putty-infilled' with heavy foundation that accentuated the crows feet around their eyes and furrowed foreheads, wrinkled necks exaggerated by low-cut tops, thickened waists dripping with chain-belts and fake-gold jewellery, these women looked and sounded utterly ridiculous. Never mind mutton! They were dead sheep dressed as spring lambs. All of them thought they looked the cat's whiskers and believed they only had to step outside preening and reverting, mentally at least, to their youthful personae to have the bees hurling themselves at these wanna-be honey pots.

Inside the hall, gangs of balding men clung to their pints as, eyes on stalks, they viewed the 'girls' emerging from their harem. I crept sideways against the wall trying to melt into the background – an instant wallflower. Many of these men reeked with a heavy and stifling mixture of aftershave, alcohol and smoke. You could suss out the stink from ten feet away. Most were dressed like ageing hippies, their shirts tucked in, their kipper ties bearing gaudy mottos, and their slightly short, flared-bottom trousers revealing the gap between hairy legs and cartoon-character socks. I promise I'm not exaggerating. These men were real 'saddos'. I stood on the perimeters of that dance floor, wondering what the blazes I was doing there. And I knew that although this mode of partner-seeking may be fine for some, it was certainly NOT for me. I felt like a cow in a cattle market. I never again went to any event where I suspected I might not feel comfortable.

Tried and tested routes

Work

OK. So it sounds clichéd. You may think you know everyone at work, from the managing director to the tea-girl. There may not even be anyone else in your workplace in your social circle or age band. If someone at work asks to date you, check out they're not married *before* you get involved. Are you courting problems? Christmas parties can be dangerous for working colleagues too. But work can be a great place to make initial contacts and thus widen your social circle.

Recent research has shown that going out for a drink with people from work not only makes for a happier but also healthier office. It is also a great way to socialise. How often do you turn down the chance on the basis that everyone else at work is younger than you are and those of your own generation who are married or have partners rush home? Next time the opportunity arises, take it. Even if they are not remotely suitable themselves, many of your colleagues undoubtedly have parents, relatives or friends in your age group who may well be alone and also looking for someone to share time and social activities with. Until you chat in a social environment, they may not even realise you are alone. Prove that you are a great person to have as a friend with a special charisma that makes people long to be with you, and there's no saying what might happen. The wider you spread your wings socially, the more chance you ultimately have of having some fun and possibly meeting a new date.

I met my second husband through work, although I didn't work with him. People laugh when I tell them how, in my capacity as a staff journalist on a Sunday magazine supplement, I was sent to interview Peter, a dentist who was at the time working part-time as a spokesperson for the British Dental Association. It was all to do with a TV programme about the training of young dentists. I never did get the feature together

– and that's the 'tooth'. Who wants to open their paper on a Sunday morning and read about student dentists cutting open pigs heads? But fate plays strange tricks. He kept ringing to find out what had happened to the feature on which he'd lavished two precious hours of his time. I kept dodging the answer. Eventually, I told him I was going on holiday. He asked what my husband did for a living. The rest, as they say, is history.

Go dancing

Yes! You can go dancing without a partner of the opposite sex. It's more fun, of course, to go with a same-sex partner. Classes that teach line dancing, salsa dancing, country and western, ballroom and ceroc, a partner dance like a French jive, abound. Men and women of all ages go along. It's fun, it's physically good for you, it's not expensive. And you could be lucky, like Debra, aged forty-four, who had been divorced for ten years when she met her partner, Philip at a ceroc group: 'We started dancing together and found we got on fantastically,' she says. 'He asked if I would be back the following week and to my amazement, when I arrived, he was downstairs waiting for me. After that, we became regular partners. Then he asked me to have dinner with him. It was great because we both loved dancing, so there was none of that awkward: "Well I like this . . . Do you like that?" to the conversation.' Many dance classes, such as MMM – the initials stand for the Margaret Morris Movement – are nationwide and advertise in local newspapers. You can contact MMM at 49 Sunningview Avenue, Biggin Hill, Kent TN16 3BX or email them at info@margaretmorris movement.com for information about groups in your area.

Bridge and other interest groups

As I mentioned earlier, I joined a bridge club as part of my personal single-again rehabilitation plan. It may sound obvious to suggest joining an evening class run by the local authority, but why not? Although I have to say I was told recently that more single women join the car maintenance and DIY classes than men. Equally, large numbers of single men often choose to do gourmet cooking classes, and it's not just a matter of personal survival. Or perhaps it is! The golden rule, however, is *don't* choose a subject simply because it's likely to attract the opposite sex. Choose it because it's something you'd really like to do, and on the basis that you will encounter new faces and make new friends of both sexes who you might not meet in your everyday life. Once again, there can be no guarantees that your fellow students will be singles, let alone in your age range. But you may meet someone who knows someone and you could end up learning to stargaze – not necessarily in an astrology class!

The club and pub scene

You may feel you're well past the clubbing scene, and that thumping music does your head in. However, if you love 1960s and 1970s music, enjoy being in the company of those of your own age, and you're looking for a bit of simple fun, search out dedicated over-forties singles events in your local paper. Many pubs have function rooms where enterprising entrepreneurs throw regular over-forties evenings. Some of the less politically correct among us may describe them as 'granny nights', but what the hell. You don't have to be a 'granny' to love sing-alongs, discos (with real music) and pub quizzes. Almost every city, town and village has at least one nightspot dedicated to running events where over-forties can meet others in the more mature age groups.

Essex Singles, for example, is a social club for people of all ages, ranging, they say, from late twenties to early-eighties, although most of their members are in their thirties, forties and fifties. It's the brainchild of Les Ainsworth who has been running similar clubs for more than fifteen years in the Romford, Braintree, Brentwood and Basildon areas. For more information about their social events, which include dances and outings, contact Ainsworth on 01708 760247 or email les@essex-singles.co.uk. Cascade is a social club organising events for single people up to the age of fifty in the West Country. The initials stand for Caring Adults Singles Club Arranging Diverse Events. You can write to their organisers at Cascade Singles Ltd., Harlech House, Harlech Drive, Rhiwderin, Newport NP10 8QS, or call them on 01633 896506. Or visit their website at www.cascade.eu.com. There are numerous such clubs around the country and the Internet is probably the most useful way of sourcing them. Go to a search engine such as Google and put in the words: over forty singles clubs. You'll be amazed at what comes up. You don't need a computer in order to enjoy all the contact facilities the Internet can offer. Simply visit an Internet café and if you're unfamiliar with surfing, there's bound to be someone around to offer you help.

If you want the finest choice of over-fifties facilities for singles, I suggest you move to Florida in the USA where singles social clubs and events seem to abound.

Pat and Andy's 'granny night' romance

Pat was fifty-five when she met her husband Andy, then thirty-eight, at what she calls a 'granny night' held in the function room at a local hotel, near her old home in Staffordshire. Pat's no stranger to dating mid-life. Andy is husband number five:

'I was lucky because I had a single sister in the same age group and we were part of a crowd. You can't go to these things alone. We used to go to the "granny night" socials and dances held at local pubs and clubs on Thursdays, Fridays and Saturdays. I wasn't especially looking for dates. I just went along for a laugh. I've never gone out looking for a man. Women who are looking for dates smell of desperation and it puts the men off. Men find it attractive to be in the company of someone who's happy to be a friend and who's not looking to rush into a relationship. Just being yourself is what's important.'

As regulars at one particular club, Pat, her sister Kath and their friends used to make for the same table every week at one of these regular socials. The night she and Andy first met, six years ago, they walked in to find two strange men sitting in their seats. 'They were obviously much younger than us and they looked like real squares in their M & S jumpers. Not our types at all. Far too shy,' Pat laughs.

'I went up to them and said: "What are you doing sitting at our table?" My sister and I are both quite big-busted – 42 DD – and we had to push past them to sit down. I think they got quite excited. They said: "These seats haven't got your names on, you know." They were just having a laugh and a joke with us. So we joined them and chatted and thought nothing of it. Then we started sitting together every week. I discovered Andy was reliable and trustworthy, a real gentleman and not a boozer. That suited me because I don't drink. Three of my other four husbands had all been boozers and treated me very badly. Gradually, we became friends and then we fell for one another. We started going out after about three months and there were problems. There always are. He was still living at home with his mum, and she found it hard to accept me. She didn't even come to our wedding. Being an only child and never married, it took Andy a long time to fit into a big family. He can't get used to the idea that people can walk into one another's homes and help themselves to anything that's in the fridge, but that is family life. But despite all the problems, we get on great together. I still follow a lot of my own interests, like line dancing and going to night school to learn upholstery. We've bought a hotel in Blackpool and we're building a business together. I'm a big lady, but men still seem to find me interesting.

Andy is flattered by that rather than worried about it. He says he knows I'm faithful and it's great to have a wife who's in demand.'

Mid-life activity clubs

Apart from local over-forties singles nights held in function rooms or pubs, or localised social groups such as Cascade, there are a number of national social groups such as Nexus if you feel like broadening your horizons. Nexus is more than just a basic introduction agency, although it does function at 'list level'. But the lists are intended as friendship tools as well as dating vehicles and newsletters include details of events being run by members in different parts of the country, which anyone who shares a similar interest can join. You can meet face-to-face as well as on paper. If you are unattached, the most natural thing in the world is your desire to meet others in a similar position – not solely because you are a man or woman 'on the hunt'.

'There are many reasons that extend beyond partner-seeking,' says Nexus' joint founder, Barbara Holt Bright. 'Just look at it this way. If you played golf, you could walk down the street past ten other golfers, but would you know who they were? To find out, you would have to go to where they congregate and be recognised as one of them. The same applies to being an unattached person. You must go to where the others are – and that's where Nexus comes in.' The Nexus umbrella encompasses not just Britain but the world through Nexus International. There are members in Australia, Germany, Iraq, the Philippines, Lithuania, Italy, South Africa and Northern Ireland. Contact them at Nexus House, 6 The Quay, Bideford, North Devon EX39 2HW for further details, or call them on 01237 471704.

WLTM – the lonely hearts columns

Lonely hearts columns are a great way to meet new people. Many national and most local papers have a weekly section, as do special interest magazines. Magazines dedicated to the 'silver' market such as *Yours* and *The Saga Magazine* also carry advertisements aimed specifically at mid-life singles looking for romance, although you will, of course, find ads aimed at older people dotted among the generally younger ones in magazines such as *Time Out*.

If you decide to place or answer an advert:

- *Do* advertise in, or answer an ad in, a newspaper or magazine you would choose to read, rather than in a publication you would never touch if you weren't scouring the lonely hearts columns.
- *Look behind the jargon* for clues about the advertiser. Many who advertise their personal qualities have apparently learned their promotional techniques from estate agents. They tell half the truth, omit design problems, forget to mention that the foundations may be slipping a bit or that the 'property' would be a darned sight more attractive if it had a lick of paint to freshen it up.
- *Be outrageous if you dare*. Some ads are memorable for their outrageousness. I'll never forget one I spotted once with the headline: *Roses and New Potatoes*. I wish I'd kept it because it read along the lines of: 'Flower-loving fifty-year-old academic seeks confident country woman for walks, talks, cycling and swimming. Animal lover – Scottish and Welsh replies particularly welcome.' He omitted the clichéd requirement for a g.s.o.h. (good sense of humour) but one supposes he must either have had a v.g.s.o.h. – or been totally humour deficient. I just had visions of this slightly paunchy gentleman roaming the Welsh hills or alongside Scottish burns, his academic cape fluttering in the gentle breeze and his mortar board held firmly in place on his greying and

balding head with Velcro, a bunch of thornless roses firmly wedged behind ear, as he calls to Shep, Rover and the other three canine friends who accompany him everywhere.

This is just a tongue-in-cheek rough guide of how to read some of these ads, especially if you're playing the advertising game for the first time:

When men advertise

- Handsome male – women should read 'if you like a man who takes longer than you preening in the bathroom'
- Sincere and charming – obsequious
- Intelligent – can read
- Charismatic – likes to take centre stage at every opportunity
- Genuine – well he told the truth when he said he was male
- Al Pacino look-alike – vain bastard with an inflated sense of his star quality

When women advertise

- Very attractive, sexy – men should read 'wears dresses cut to her waist, skirts that are little more than belts'.
- Curvaceous – overweight
- Occasional smoker – chain puffer
- N/S – and don't you dare light the occasional cigar either
- Tall – 6'3" without heels
- With stamina – she's a bit of a 'goer' and will pounce
- Earth mother – straggly grey hair, flowing embroidered peasant robes and still flower-powered out

Angela's experience

No matter how choosy you are about the ads you reply to, and even after taking all possible precautions, responding to ads can prove a rather haphazard business.

Angela, forty-nine, answered an ad in her local newspaper that promised an 'Intelligent n/s [non-smoking] professional forty-something male w.l.t.m. [would like to meet] attractive female with view to friendship, maybe more.'

Angela describes her experience:

'We chatted for hours on the phone and arranged to meet in a local restaurant. He was already sitting at the table, looking unkempt and dishevelled when I arrived, a little the worse for the half bottle of red wine he'd already consumed. I spent the whole evening being bored witless as he regaled me with stories of his academic achievements. I didn't get a word in edgeways. He asked me if I'd like a coffee. I told him I didn't drink coffee, so he asked me what I did drink and when I said I loved a nice cup of tea, he told me he'd bring me one in bed every morning. I offered to split the bill and to his credit he declined. The restaurant had been his idea. He walked me to my car and asked me what I did for a living. I think it was the first time I had opened my mouth all evening. Then he asked me whether I owned my flat and would I mind telling him how much I earned because he just wanted to make sure I was financially independent before we got too involved. I told him I minded very much, slammed the door and drove off. He rang and left a message on the answering machine to invite me out again. Needless to say, I didn't reply.'

Writing an ad

There's an art to writing successful newspaper dating ads. The more people you attract, the more chance you have of finding someone who's right for you.

- Make the first few words punchy, but not 'off the wall'. Say something different that will offer a clue to your character. Going back to our *Roses and New Potatoes* example (it was for real – I promise), it suggests a man who will bring flowers and is possibly into organic gardening. It was certainly different enough to catch my attention.
- Describe yourself briefly, including the colour of your hair and eyes.
- Give a brief description of your character. Are you reliable, sympathetic, a good listener?
- If everyone else is advertising themselves as attractive, intelligent, educated, tall, short, caring, affectionate, or that inevitable g.s.o.h., think about what it is that makes you unique and flaunt it. There are millions of attractive/handsome, caring/affectionate, family-minded men/women looking for a partner who likes travel/walking/talking/swimming/dining-out/theatre/animals/the country. If you collect butterflies or enjoy hot-air ballooning or abseiling, say so. Show a bit of charisma and spirit. It should be a tease to encourage someone with similar interests and opinions to reply.
- Keep your ad short and to the point. You'll have a chance to say more on your telephone follow-up (more tips on that next).
- Be as honest as you can be in twenty words.
- Don't request the impossible because it sounds good. Most advertisers claim they w.l.t.m. a professional man or woman. By so doing they are severely limiting their choices. There is a (false) notion that professional people always tend to be better heeled, better mannered and better spoken than their non-professional brothers and sisters but that's not entirely true. There are many poor, badly mannered professionals and plenty of bright, intelligent non-academics and business people out there looking for love. Be prepared to broaden your horizons.

Recording a message

When you place an advertisement in any publication, you will almost certainly be invited to record a telephone message, which will be your next point of contact with your respondents.

- Do write down all the points you want to expand on.
- Do write out your self-appraisal, detailing your occupation, your interests and hobbies so that you can remind yourself of all the things you enjoy. If you love to dance, say so. Do you love or hate politics and/or pets? Do you belong to any particular groups or societies? Is religion important to you, and if so, which faith do you follow? Are you an outdoor type?

You might say something like: 'I'm forty-five, a radiologist and I love the great outdoors. I'm financially independent and own my own flat in (supply area). I love sunshine holidays, jazz and big show band music, particularly the score of *Chicago*. I have independent adult children and a large circle of loving friends and a pet poodle called Pooch. I'm a carnivore and love to eat a good steak. I'm a great cook but enjoy eating out. However I hate Thai and Chinese food. I enjoy children, but having brought up my own two, I don't really want to meet a man with a young family. I hope to meet someone who will share my passion for hill walking, initially for friendship and maybe more. Please leave me your number.' (*Women, note: never give out a landline number if you can possibly help it. Always offer your mobile.*)

You've now shown that you're an independent, educated, sociable family person with an appealing personality, who loves a certain kind of music, and certain kinds of holidays. There's still plenty to say when you get to speak to one another.

- Do make notes but don't *read* your self-description into the phone or you will lose spontaneity in your voice. Try your response into a tape recorder before you record it down the

phone. Check the modulation of your voice. Make it sound bright and friendly and try to avoid sounding high-pitched and squeaky.
- Do keep it to less than forty-five seconds. Anything longer can be boring.

Answering an advert

You may prefer to answer an advert than place one. If the written word is attractive and the voice appeals, then do:

- Tell the advertiser a little bit about yourself (being as honest as you can). Again it might help if you jot down a few notes so that you can refer to them as you speak. If you read your reply, it will sound stilted, so try to make it appear more spontaneous.
- Offer a landline number for the advertiser to reply to if you're a man – but a mobile number only if you're female.
- Women should ALWAYS ring the man back to ensure he's given her the right name and number.
- Have at least two telephone conversations before you arrange to meet, to get to know one another a little.
- Women should always be sure to tell a friend who she is meeting, when and where. She should also arrange to call her friend when she gets home to let her know she's safe. If she's in any doubt, ask a couple to pop along and have a drink quietly at the place where you've arranged to meet. That way, you have a double safety back-up, and good friends will always be happy to help. If all goes well, you can always introduce them through the 'fancy meeting you here' routine.
- Never invite a strange man to collect you at home. Always arrange to meet in a mutually convenient public place.
- Do arrange to meet for coffee or a drink on a first date, rather than dinner. That way you won't need to feel guilty if you don't want to see him/her again and there will be no awkwardness about who pays the bill.

Christine's experience

Christine is fifty-six and often places adverts in the Kindred Spirits section of the *Daily Telegraph*. That she has done so several times suggests that she hasn't found it a particularly successful way of dating yet, but she says she has a lot of fun sorting out the replies and that she widens her horizons by meeting as many men as she can. She says:

> 'The biggest problem is that at this age, you don't meet people naturally as you do when you are younger. And in my experience, another problem at this age is that all the nice men are married! So if you do meet a single man, you have to stop and think. Is he someone else's reject?
>
> 'When a man has been granted custody of his children or if his children have chosen to live with him, that is always a good sign. I prefer to place the ads rather than respond to the ads other people place, because that way you lay out what it is you are looking for. I wrote out the last one I did at about three one morning. I started it by saying something like "Nigel Havers look-alike wanted but willing to compromise." There are some nice men out there and I've met some very interesting people. The first time I placed an ad, a gentleman rang me from Cyprus. Obviously that was not dating-range, but I've got a lovely friend and if I ever get out there, I'll get in touch.'

Judith's story

Judith has placed adverts on a number of occasions. She too prefers to be a 'placer' rather than a 'responder'. But she emphasises how vital it is to spend time chatting to respondents on the phone before meeting. 'I had a couple of very pleasant chats with one particular man,' she says. 'He knew I was a professional lady and during our second conversation, he asked me how much I earned. I told him it was none of his bloody business. I was delighted we chatted for long enough for me to discover that he was after my money, before we met. At least we didn't waste time.'

Social clubs

There are some truly amazing opportunities to meet people with similar interests and to enjoy a great time pursuing a favourite hobby, or a new experience that could become a favourite if only you know where to look. If you've ever fancied abseiling, canoeing, white-water rafting, climbing, water skiing or bungee jumping, now's the time to go for it. Although not aimed merely at singles, a large proportion of those who belong to Spice UK are alone, and the age range varies from twenty-somethings to sixty-somethings, so it's worth investigating. You can find them on the Internet at www.spiceuk.com or at Spice UK, 13 Thorpe St., Old Trafford, Manchester M16 9PR; telephone: 0161 873 8788.

Northern Link, run by Karen Seddon (26 Fryent Close, Blackrod, Bolton BL6 5BU; telephone: 01204 460 989; email karen.nl@ic24.net) sponsor a whole range of events across the north of England, from walks to ballroom and modern sequence dancing classes, drink 'n' chat nights, pub quiz nights and theatre outings across the north of England. They've even got a 'matching' service, Connections, that offers to link members through a confidential matching service.

4

Agency dating and other adventures

If you have made a determined, conscious decision to find a lifetime partner, then it makes sense to seek a partner in places where other people are making serious and similarly enthusiastic efforts. And when people are prepared to spend what often amounts to impressive sums of money to find an appropriate mate, it is reasonable to assume that they're as serious about succeeding in their mission as you are.

God helps those who help themselves

If you're having second thoughts about even reading this chapter, take a long hard look at how life is right now. If you're happy living alone without love at what should be the most rewarding time of your whole life, then why are you reading this book? A recent survey showed that informal live-in relationships are generally short-lived. If you're fed up with changing partners and would dearly love to find a man or woman with whom you can spend the rest of your life, read on. But if you truly intend to 'have a go' at finding love in the middle of your life, then the only person who can really help you is YOU. If you don't have a friend who can introduce you to your ideal mate, why not pay a professional to be your friend and help you along the way? Years ago, there was a stigma to paying an agency to introduce you to a partner. Today, more and more people are doing it – and the majority of those who join are busy, professional, mid-life people who don't have the time or inclination to try the hit-and-miss methods we've already discussed.

Ask yourself:

- Am I waiting for other people to introduce me to someone?
- Do I fancy adding a bit of excitement and adding a little spice to my life?
- Am I game for a bit of fun?
- Do I want to widen my social circle?
- Am I courageous enough to really go out and find the man or woman who will complete my life?
- Do I believe that I am ultimately responsible for my own fate?

If you can answer yes to at least four of the above, then you are ready to take control. You may be led into avenues you never expected to explore. There may be times when you may wonder why you're even bothering. As Shakespeare said: 'The course of true love never did run smooth.' But if you don't go for it yourself, you can't expect other people to do it for you.

Dating and introduction agencies

Does the very thought of signing up with an introduction or dating agency make you shudder? It did me, once upon a time, but now I'm not sure why. After all, you wouldn't be embarrassed to meet a potential partner as a result of an introduction by a mutual friend, would you? You'd probably be happy to go on a blind date with a friend of a friend. And, you wouldn't think twice about using an employment agency to find a new job or fill an office vacancy with an appropriate employee. So when there's a vacancy for a partner to share your life from this day forward, what's wrong with seeking professional help and empowering them to act as your 'match-making friend'? You only need to browse through the pages of upmarket women's magazines such as *The Tatler* or even *Time Out* to discover how popular introduction and dating services have become.

Robert Epstein, editor of the prestigious US magazine *Psychology Today*, believes that the Western reliance on spontaneous passion as a basis for lifelong commitment is not, in fact, the worldwide norm. 'Sixty per cent of the world's marriages are not love marriages,' he says. 'They're arranged. Arranged marriage demonstrates that people can learn to love.' This is an interesting concept coming from such a learned source. For years, critics have condemned arranged marriages as practised in Eastern cultures and in orthodox Jewish circles. Now, a responsible and world-respected psychologist is reaching the same positive conclusion that several of the world's greatest religions and cultures have been propounding for years. A fully comprehensive list of dating agencies can be found on www.whichintro.com, a website founded by Penrose and Bill Halson. Penrose Halson ran the Katharine Allen marriage bureau for many years. Her husband is an experienced business consultant and counsellor and a former chairman of the National Family Trust, which works to help couples about to embark on a new relationship or revitalise an old one. They started the website to provide a comprehensive database of the 250-plus introduction agencies in the UK, providing honest, accurate and up-to-date information about these agencies to members who pay £20 a year for this and a range of other services.

There's a world of difference between marriage bureaux and dating and introduction agencies. Don't make the mistake of believing they're all the same. The difference is very often reflected in the price.

Marriage bureaux

Most (though not all) marriage bureaux offer the highest level of personal service and are aimed at those who are really serious about wanting to marry. They generally charge accordingly. You might expect to pay upwards of £1000 to a reputable agency for a year's membership, but it could be a worthwhile investment in your own future. Choose a reputable agency. If you pay a large sum up-front, you can be fairly sure that so have the people you are likely to meet, and it's fair to assume that they really are seeking a permanent relationship. Expect to attend for at least one personal interview. You will be required to fill in an extensive questionnaire and it is likely that you will be asked not only for proof of your identity, such as a passport, but also to provide utility bills in your own name to show that you are who you say you are. Very often, marriage bureaux will also ask for referees, possibly your local vicar, priest or doctor. Expect to make a further payment if a wedding is arranged.

Dating agencies

These agencies will take personal charge of your 'case', although the people who join are interested more in finding partners and less in the commitment of marriage. You will be invited to fill in a lengthy and quite detailed questionnaire and the best agencies also insist that you attend a personal interview. This is merely a means of ensuring that you look like your picture, that you are who you say you are, and that you match the description you give of yourself. The company's trained employees will then hand-match individuals to others. They may use computers too, to hone down interests and so on. But you can be almost certain that if you go on a date, your date will have been carefully chosen on the basis of what both of you have said. These agencies are expensive and registration with one can range upwards from £400 to £800 a year. Some expect a further payment if you wish to marry the person to whom they have introduced you. Most carry out security checks on their clients before taking their money, again often via utility bills.

Introduction agencies

These can vary from what appear to be little more than DIY schemes where you are provided with a list of vague details of people in your area in return for a small fee, to amazingly complicated and complex enterprises where you fill in a detailed questionnaire which may require you to divulge everything you know about yourself, and possibly some things you've yet to discover, from the preferred colour of your undies (well almost) to whether you prefer shiatsu to Dalmatians. These details are allegedly fed into brilliant computers that can sift and sort and come up with a perfect, guaranteed, copper-bottomed and gold-plated match. You are guaranteed a minimum number of contacts (they *don't* guarantee dates – well how could they?), and some of these agencies charge enormous sums of money, although others are happy to include your details from as little as £25 for three months' membership. Some of these agencies carry out detailed security checks on their members to ensure that they are who they say they are and that the people on their books are genuine singles seeking partners.

Always pay for any fees for any of the above by credit card. This way, if they go out of business, or fail to keep their promises, you can claim your money back in exactly the same way, as credit cards indemnify you against business failures.

It's worth checking to see whether any agency you sign on with is a member of the Association of British Introduction Agencies. In 1976/77, the Office of Fair Trading responded to public anxiety and carried out a study of marriage bureaux and dating agencies. It drew up a list of basic principles of good practice and encouraged agencies to regulate themselves. The ABIA was formed in 1981 as a result and their members abide by a strict code of conduct.

According to Linda Davis, Chairperson of the ABIA, there is a great North/South divide. Although many agencies in the north of England are happy to enlist ladies over forty-five, many of those in the south have very few men of a similar age on their books. Many agencies attract far more women than men and as we have seen in chapter 1, by the age of fifty-five, it is estimated that there are eleven times more women than men looking for a relationship, largely due to different rates of birth and mortality in men and women.

If you are thinking about joining any marriage, introduction or dating agency do *check that they belong to the ABIA*. You will find the definitive list, updated daily, on the whichintro website. Their address is www.whichintro.com.

Check that:

- They have been in operation for more than two years.
- They operate a basic code of conduct for members.
- They have members in your age group.
- They are members of the Association of British Introduction Agencies or have applied for membership of that body. If you are unsure of an agency's status, check with the ABIA by contacting them at 35 Market Street, Tamworth, Staffs B19 7LR; telephone: 0845 345 2242; email enquiries@ abia.org.uk, or you could visit their website and check them out on www.whichintro.com.
- They are willing to put you in touch with others who have successfully used their services in the past.
- They cover the area where you live. It's no use if most of the agencies' members are in Aberdeen and you live in Dorset!
- The level of service they are offering. Do they have a social activities programme? How often?

- They can indicate success rates, i.e. how many couples do they know who met as a direct result of their intervention?
- Their database is large enough to offer you a reasonable chance. If it's a regional agency, between 400 and 500 names should be sufficient. You could spend £50 to meet 50 members, or possibly £100 to be offered the opportunity of contact with several thousand. How many people can they *guarantee* to introduce you to? The answer should be a minimum of six before you decide to part with your cash.
- They will tell you what time spans membership covers (i.e. three months, six months, twelve months). How many lists can you expect to receive in that time?
- They will supply you with an out-of-date list of their members so that you can get an idea of the kind of people on their books.

Although no one can guarantee who is going to join what and when, agencies should be able to offer an 'average' for the number of people on their books who might be compatible. Nor can anyone unreservedly promise you chemistry with another person. But you do need to be sure that you will receive at least a certain number of reasonably suitable introductions. If they can't supply a guaranteed number, will they extend the membership?

DON'T
- Use an agency that relies on postal questionnaires.
- Join an agency that is not prepared to give you details of its fees on the phone or in literature.
- Part with any membership fees before you have visited and had a chat with the agency. Ask for a reference if you wish. Although many good agencies are not members of the ABIA, and membership should not be used as the eleventh commandment when deciding where to go for help, members of ABIA are required to keep within a code of moral guidelines.

Wendy's experience

Wendy, forty-four, was attracted by a dating agency ad in *Time Out*. It said nothing about age-limits. 'They were happy to take all my details and to put me on their books "for computer matching" in return for what I considered to be a reasonable fee,' she says.

'The idea that I might find my match from among the countless men the agency claimed they had on their books in my age and intellectual range was tempting. In return for my money, I received a list. A long, long list it's true, but as I began to read through the personal details of these people, I realised there was not one single man on the list who fitted my criteria. For a start, most of them were in their twenties and thirties. Of those in my age group, few were the sort of man I was happy to meet: I wanted to meet a cultured gentleman who would share my love of theatre and classical concerts. Most of the people on the list were more interested in hiking and outdoor pursuits. Not my scene at all. I met one man who sounded very acceptable on paper. We went to an outdoor Gilbert and Sullivan concert. He spent the evening telling me how his marriage went wrong and why his children would not speak to him any more, and how he was very short of money because his ex was fleecing him for every penny he had not yet earned. He refused to expand on the "business" activities in which he was engaged, although he seemed most anxious to discover my sources of income. It poured with rain and, huddling under an umbrella with him, I realised that he lacked a lot in the personal hygiene department. It was then that I conceded that an introduction agency can be a hit and miss affair, especially where over-forties are concerned.

Agencies for the more mature

There are a number of sound introduction agencies run specifically for mature people, but too many to list individually. One such, Autumn Friends (telephone 01874 636909), was started by Polly Langford, forty-seven, who is a member of the Association of British Introduction Agencies. Langford actually runs two agencies side-by-side, Autumn Friends and Woodland Friends, which has country people as its main target audience. Woodland Friends is aimed at twenties to forties; Autumn Friends specifically targets the mature market of forty-five plus.

'I started a general introduction agency aimed at country people aged between twenty and fifty, but then I realised that single people in the older age groups often find meeting others of a similar age fraught with difficulties. Many tried to sign up with us but were fed up with finding only younger people on the monthly lists I send out. And I discovered something else. Some of the widowed ladies said they would be quite interested in meeting other widowed ladies. Many had nursed sick husbands for years and got out of the habit of living a social life and they wanted female friends with whom they could start to build a social life again. Older men, however, were generally only interested in meeting women. That's when I thought it might be a good idea to split my agency into two groups – so now Autumn Friends is aimed at those in their forties and fifties although we do have people on our mailing lists up to the age of eighty-five, and Woodland Friends targets the younger age group.

'I charge £50 for three months' membership during which time they can expect to receive four lists of members' names. Six months' membership costs £75 and members get seven lists. People who join for a year pay £100 and will receive 13 lists with first names and details of other members in the same age group. All the members write their own profiles. If

I were to try to meet every member, it would make the costs prohibitive and I do like to try to keep them reasonable. Each one has a box number so they can write to one another through the agency initially, and they can include phone numbers if they wish to do so. However, many older people have preconceived ideas of what is "right". One of the commonest problems I face is that older women tend to be inhibited about contacting men and insist on waiting for men to make the first move. Today, it is perfectly acceptable for women to make the first call. It's all about overcoming inbred inhibitions. I probably get between four and five real matches a year. I think one of the cutest things that happened was the man in his sixties who loved caravanning and who became friendly with a lady in her fifties who also loved caravanning. They lived several counties apart so they arranged to meet in a caravan park and parked their caravans side-by-side. Unfortunately, it didn't work long-term.

'Of course, we meet all sorts. There was this ex-military gentleman in his seventies who said that ladies never responded to his letters. Then I discovered he was telling the women he corresponded with that he had a lovely house set in its own grounds. He thought that was enough to persuade hoards of them to rush to live with him as his housekeeper and thought it was a marvellous offer. He could not believe that women today often had houses of their own and I tried to explain that most women who join an introduction agency are looking for a little more than just somewhere pleasant to live in return for being unpaid housekeepers.'

DO

Check the level of service every agency you approach offers and make sure you are fully cognisant with the eventual cost.

Lunch and dinner dating

Lunch dating

Lunch dating is one of the newest innovations to appear on the dating scene from the USA. This is arranged dating but with a difference, and if you're a full-time career or professional person, it offers a golden opportunity to meet new people of the opposite sex within a 'time-limit' atmosphere. The beauty of it is that there are none of the strings that can sometimes be attached to a one-to-one blind-date dinner. It is perfectly safe because the restaurant staff is fully aware of what is going on. You leave at the end of the meal (which you pay for yourself) with no commitment to call your lunch date. Whether or not you decide you want to meet again is entirely your choice and you need say nothing. That's done for you by the organisers and is all part of the service. Mary Balfour, who runs Only Lunch as well as the more conventional introduction agency Drawing Down the Moon and the website loveandfriends.com, from her office at Adam and Eve Mews, 165 Kensington High Street, London W8 6SH (telephone 0207 376 2213), explains:

> 'Only Lunch is aimed at busy professionals and all our clients are interviewed personally. We insist on ID and proof that the would-be luncher is free to date. Then we rely on a mixture of experience and instinct to match our lunch dates. We are much better at introducing like-minded people than well-meaning but inexperienced relatives and friends.'

When a couple have been matched, the agency book a table for two at an upmarket restaurant. You can choose what you eat and you pay for it yourself, so there's no awkwardness about ordering whatever you fancy and wondering what will happen when the bill arrives. The advantages over blind dinner-dating one-to-one are:

- Because one or both of you are working, time is limited so there's no embarrassment about carrying the date on longer when the meal is over or inviting anyone to join you in a nightcap, because you both have somewhere else to go to.
- There is no need to exchange telephone numbers or details at the end of the meal. The agency provides a questionnaire that both parties complete afterwards to find out how you got on and will only pass on contact details with your permission.

'Some people who find lunching during the week difficult may find weekend lunch dates more convenient,' says Mary Balfour. 'Others prefer an early supper. However, whichever way they choose to do it, we do put a time limit on the meal. If people are getting on really well, they can, of course, ignore it, but it gives people the perfect get-out without appearing rude.'

Only Lunch charge £895 including VAT, which ensures a minimum of eight lunch dates within a year, although they say they often offer more for the older age groups who may have 'more problems' finding a compatible mate. They offer £100 discount if someone agrees to join at the time of their first interview. Although Only Lunch is based in London, there are other similar lunch clubs nationwide. Look out for advertisements in national magazines, *Time Out* local editions and local newspapers.

Dinner dates

How do you like going out for dinner? Is a romantic meal in good company one of the things you miss terribly in your single life? Of course, being single doesn't mean you can't enjoy a well-cooked restaurant meal, but sharing such a meal with other couples or same-sex friends doesn't have quite the same feel about it as when you're wining and dining with an attractive member of the opposite sex. If you haven't got one particular partner to go with, have you ever thought of going on a dinner date with a group of other men and women who are also single, mid-life and seeking love?

When you go dinner dating, you will find yourself in a room with some twenty or thirty other guests. Most dinner-dating agencies try to arrange for equal numbers of men and women. You get to enjoy a fine meal in the company of other people who are alone, and most dinner-dating agencies arrange these meals in age brackets. *But do be honest about your age when you book, for your own sake as well as everyone else's.* While it may be fun to be able to blend with all these young things, you can be sure that you will give yourself away sooner or later. And your fellow diners who may have paid a hefty price for the meal and the chance to meet a mate will not be happy bunnies if they feel they've been duped – any more than you might be, if you unexpectedly found yourself out of your own age range.

Agencies that arrange dinner-dating parties currently flourish throughout the UK. The idea of dinner dating with a crowd of strangers may sound daunting, but it does have a number of advantages as a way of finding a partner. Some people are happy to go along to such an event for the first time with a same-sex friend for Dutch courage, but that can have disadvantages. First of all, you might both end up fancying the same person. Secondly, you might find yourself constrained by being with someone else if there's the prospect of a coffee or drink afterwards with a convivial partner. Thirdly, there is always the fear that they may be successful and you may not (or vice-versa). *If you can find the courage to go along alone, do so.* Take a taxi there and back (look on it as part of the investment) so that you can relax and enjoy a glass of wine (or three).

Finding a dinner-dating venue in your area is not as difficult as it sounds. Most Sunday broadsheet newspapers and up-market magazines, including *The Tatler, Time Out, Harpers and Queen* and *The Lady*, carry advertisements for such events. Ring the organisers listed to find out more. Perhaps one of the best-known agencies for dinner dating is Dinner Dates, originally started in London in 1989 by Hillie Marshall and currently running as a franchise operation across the UK. For details of your nearest branch contact Dinner Dates Ltd., 8 Millers Court, Chiswick Mall, London W4 2PF, or take a look at their website, www.dinnerdates.com. In London, they host parties at such venues as The Ritz, Claridges, The Elephant on the River and the Kensington Roof Gardens. Obviously cost varies according to venue – but as you might expect, they don't come cheap. Local franchised parties are run at equally upmarket venues around Great Britain.

I went along to one of the earliest parties, at the beginning of the 1990s, and must admit I felt quite awkward walking into a room full of total strangers. At that time, Hillie Marshall herself was the hostess. With a name badge bravely attached to my posh frock and a glass of wine in my hand, I entered the fray. After introductions and cocktails, the ladies were seated at what were to be their places for the evening. The gentlemen moved with each course. The food was not bad (I have to put my hand on my heart and admit I have tasted better), and the quality of the male company varied from boring and boorish to just about acceptable. I didn't fancy a single one of the men who were present that night, although a couple made it plain they fancied me! Perhaps it was just a bad night. Others I know who have done it have had more rewarding experiences. I looked on the whole thing as a bit of a laugh, and put it down to experience on the basis that at least it might provide some material for a future feature in a book or magazine!

Dining clubs

With dinner dates, you buy a one-off meal at a venue of your choice. However, dinner clubbing is a slightly different variation on the theme. With dinner clubbing, you buy membership to a special-interest dinner club, often within an age range so you can be sure to have at least a couple of things in common when you turn up for the first time. There are hundreds of such clubs dotted around the British Isles and aligned to other agencies, from singles holiday organisations to social clubs. Perhaps one of the most innovative of these dinner-dating clubs is ClubSix, whose offices are based at 152–160 City Road, London EC1V 2NX. Joint-founder Don Koulaouzos says:

'We don't look on ClubSix as a dating or introduction service. There are no strings at any of our events. We spent six months researching the product we sell before we launched our service in 1994. We don't ask our clients to fill in complicated psychometric testing forms. We believe these are only one-dimensional and while they're a fine way of matching job seekers to employment, we don't consider them useful in the meeting game. When people fill in forms, they're under pressure. What we want to provide is an environment where successful people can go to meet one another while enjoying a perfectly natural way of socialising – a meal where six people, three of each sex, sit round a table and enjoy a meal together. Six is a number that works perfectly. It's large enough to allow for a little interpersonal freedom, yet small enough for intimacy and the chance to really get to know your fellow diners.'

ClubSix caters for every age from twenty plus. However, there are dedicated over-forties dinners, complete with themes. If you choose to join this group, or a similar one, don't worry: ClubSix say the bulk of their members are in their forties and fifties and they do aim some of their themed dinners particularly at mature men and women, so that like meets like. ClubSix have developed what they describe as a unique series of eight personal group profile themes. Koulaouzos explains:

'We act as our clients' personal social secretaries in bringing six people, three men and three women, of similar ages and interests, together round a dinner table in the kind of restaurant they would choose to dine at under any circumstances.

So, for example, if you like fine dining, aged wines and interesting venues while enjoying good company, you might choose one of our Dining and Night Life parties. If you love to keep up-to-date with the latest films or theatrical productions and enjoy art and literature, you could plump for an Arts and Entertainment night. Our Business and Technology evenings are aimed at those who are looking for new opportunities to enjoy the world of commerce and industry and can't wait to lay their hands on the latest gadgets. We also have Sport and Adventure dinners and Outdoors and Nature theme evenings.'

Membership of ClubSix isn't cheap. You can give it a one-off whirl for a £45 temporary membership fee plus the cost of the meal. Or you might join the Premium Membership scheme for £215 a year plus £15 for each event you attend, plus the cost of dinner. There are other options in between. 'When people come to me and say, "I haven't met the right person", I tell them, "The danger of looking for the perfect person is that when you do think you've found them, they too will be looking for the perfect person and in all probability, it won't be you," ' Koulaouzos says.

Speed dating

Speed dating arrived in Britain from the USA in early 2002. Aish HaTorah, an international Jewish educational network, created speed dating two years ago and it took off in America as various entrepreneurs recognised the advantages such a system offered all singles as a means to make new friends and possibly find love. When Miranda, a character in *Sex and the City*, the seminal American comedy about finding love in the urban jungle, went speed dating, it led to a rash of copycat firms springing up. In Britain, it was initially aimed at twenty-something professionals, but it has proved so popular that the age groups are expanding and now include forty- and fifty-somethings too. Speed Daters, one of several companies who've entered the speed-dating business are expanding to include forties and fifties evenings. They hire an upmarket hall or bar and invite twenty applicants within the age group – ten men and ten women. The women are given letters and the men numbers. They all have cards with three columns, one for first name, one for 'yes' and one signifying 'no'. Lady 'A' meets gentleman '1' at a table numbered '1'. They chat for three minutes. A bell rings. They mark their cards according to whether they might be interested in seeing that person again for a proper chat or not. Gentleman '2' moves to meet Lady 'A', and so it goes on – for two hours. At the end of the evening, the cards are collected. The organisers sort out where two 'yes's' coincide, contact the speed daters, and pass on details. The evening could well result in several dates – or of course none at all. But apparently, and although Speed Daters has been going for a relatively short time, organiser Simon says he has several regulars intent on coming back for more. If you would like to try this exciting (and I have to say precarious-sounding) new medium, contact Speed Daters on 08702 430935, or visit their website at www.speeddater.co.uk for details of speed-dating events around Britain.

Singles breaks and holidays

In my mid-life single days, I did go on several holidays alone. This was at a time when all my married friends, freed for the first time in years from the constraints of childcare and school holidays, were taking off for weekends away and holidays in exotic places. I admit it: I was jealous. Not a nice trait to discover in oneself. I'm grateful that some of my closest friends invited me to share their breaks and included me warmly, but, yet again, I felt the odd one out on these weekends. The venues were not of my choosing. All too often, I was forced to pay the appalling 'singles supplement' which often amounted to a third as much again on the cost of my break (and holiday). Where can a single forty-something go alone for a break in cold, wet, windy Britain, or on a European hop? After adventuring down the west coast of America virtually alone and taking myself from the top to the toe of Israel, I decided I'd had enough of lone tours abroad. I decided to book a singles holiday.

At that time, my only choice was to book with Solos, a northwest London-based firm who had the foresight to realise the problems faced by the mature lone traveller. Now there are a number of companies who claim to specialise in different kinds of holidays for singles in their forties and fifties. The Internet is a great source of information. You might try visiting Club55 at www.travel55.co.uk, which features a whole number of ideas including a range of singles holidays for this age group. Solitair of 40 Princess Street, Manchester M1 6DE, telephone 0161 234 0080, are just one of those featured on the site. They say they manage to offer their tour groups intimacy on trips to Barbados, Thailand, Greece, Italy, Vietnam and Indonesia, all without the bugbear of the singles supplement. 'We choose small, family-run hotels who understand the special needs of our customers,' they say.

Singles of all ages now have a wide range of choice for short-break holidays, both in the UK and abroad. Several North American firms offer equally enticing holidays in the USA, the Caribbean and exotic destinations worldwide. For further information on a huge range of US-based holidays, as well as on international singles groups, both religious and general interest, and those specifically aimed at the mature market, visit www.singlesonthego.com. The lists there appear endless. The best news about almost 99 per cent of these vacations is that singles supplements don't apply. So, whether you're looking for a golfing weekend or a trip on the Orient Express, you will almost certainly be able to find a trip that appeals in the company of people in the same age group and situation as yourself. Other companies specialising in singles holidays for the mature include Small World (0870 576 8373) and Travel One 0870 757 2488; www.travelone.co.uk. If you are having problems booking a suitable single holiday, you might also contact the Single Travellers Action Group (STAG) which was set up by widow Jean Jewell after the death of her husband in 1993, to counter the problems faced by single travellers. 'Everyone knows about racism, sexism and ageism,' she says. 'But what about "singleism"? STAG is campaigning for government action on the issue and now has more than two thousand members nationwide.' The group produces a newsletter three times a year with details of supplement-free holidays. For further information, contact them at Church Lane, Sharnbrook, Bedford, Beds MK44 1HR.

But can you realistically expect to meet and date – and possibly mate – as a result of a singles holiday? Of course, there's nothing to it when you're sweet sixteen or even sophisticated twenty-six. Pluck up the courage and book a singles holiday, and you could have just as much fun in your forties, fifties or sixties as you did at twenty-one, even if you don't find the love of your life. Gill Harvey, MD of Solo's holidays says: 'People who take part know before they embark on one of our holidays, whether it's in Britain or abroad, that the people they are travelling with will not only be in the same age group, but will also share the same interests as themselves,' she says.

Harvey insists that the holidays are not intended as dating vehicles, although she and her staff try to balance their male/female ratio in the name of achieving the kind of normality that so many single people miss so desperately.

'We try to balance the sexes out, although it's not always possible. However, if we find that a particular holiday seems to be attracting a totally unrealistic ratio of women to men, we try to warn all travellers in advance and offer them the opportunity to change their plans if they wish. At the end of the day, most of the clients say that they are going on holiday to enjoy that holiday and share experiences with other people and make friends of both sexes. We rarely get weddings, but it does happen. And if our clients do meet someone, that is an added bonus.'

Harvey advises mature singles who are considering a singles holiday, but are unsure as to whether or not it's the right thing for them, to try a short break first before booking a longer holiday. Newcomers' weekends range from as little as £60 to around £300 for one, two or three nights as well as golfing, tennis and hiking holidays.

- Be reassured that you can join in as little or as much as you want to. There is no pressure to follow the crowd if that is not your idea of fun.
- Be aware that if you choose to go on a singles holiday, you will be broadening your horizons outside your normal social circle. You will have an opportunity to socialise on different levels with people you might otherwise never have met before.

Ken and Angela

Ken and Angela met on a Solo's holiday. Ken, now fifty-five, had been divorced for more than fifteen years at the time he booked his second singles holiday to Tenerife, and it was there that he met Angela, now sixty-one, and also a divorcee. The couple have just celebrated their third wedding anniversary, yet when they booked their holiday, neither had any thoughts about meeting a possible partner.

Angela had been taking Solo's holidays since 1992 and had been on weekend breaks to Paris and the Channel Islands as well as on longer trips abroad to destinations such as Cyprus. Their meeting was clearly fated. Angela had originally booked to go to Lanzarote, but the holiday was cancelled. She was offered a similar deal in Eilat in Israel but didn't fancy that, and plumped for the Tenerife deal only at the last minute.

Ken explains:

'In the past, I had gone on holidays with my former wife or with my partner. I went on a Saga holiday alone, and although everyone was very friendly, they were also all in couples. So when I saw a walking holiday advertised by Solo's for the forty-five plus age group on Zakynthos, one of the Greek islands, I booked. I didn't go with any expectation of meeting a lady. But I hugely enjoyed being able to go on the kind of holiday I love with other people who were of a similar age and in a similar position to myself. In the evenings, there was always company. Then I had a knee operation and decided I needed a holiday to recuperate in a warm climate, and a second trip with Solo's to Tenerife seemed like a good idea.

'I first noticed Angela in the bar where everyone met up for drinks that first evening. We had both travelled from Manchester but we'd been on different flights. I sat next to her that evening, but there was no question of pairing up. Everyone chatted with everyone else as part of the group. The hostess ran through all the trips that were available and I decided to book one or two. Angela and her friend Joan were booking at the same time the following morning and as we stood in the queue, waiting for our turn, Angela asked what I was planning to do that day. I told her I didn't know. She told me that she and her friend Joan thought they'd go into town to look around, and invited me to join them. I thought about it for about twenty minutes and then agreed that a trip around town sounded like a good idea.

'It was strange because that first day, when we went shopping, I decided to buy a suede waistcoat. When I said I liked the waistcoat, Angela said: "Why don't you buy it, then?" and Joan started laughing. Later she told us that she was sure the shop assistant thought we were married, because of the way Angela spoke to me. And although we certainly didn't pair up straight away, by the third or fourth day, it was clear we were getting on really well and I knew this could be a relationship that could go somewhere. One evening, we went to a dance place and I thoroughly enjoyed that. Then we went to the casino and that was fun too. It was obvious by this time that we really liked one another. Angela was on a later flight home than I was, so when we left on Friday afternoon, I told her I would ring her the next day. And that's what I did. We went out together on the Saturday evening. That was our first proper date.'

Angela tells her side:

'Most people who use Solo's seem to come from the south of England, so if you come from the North, as I do, keeping up any kind of relationship long distance is difficult. I never expected to meet anyone. I'd joined a dating agency at one time but I didn't enjoy the dates I met. Most of the time, they were total mismatches. I had a good job in higher management and lived in a lovely house. The men with whom I was paired off didn't realise it was heavily mortgaged and automatically assumed I was a rich widow. "I can see you are divorced but you still do your husband's books, do you?" one man said to me, on noticing the textbooks on my shelves. The insinuation was that only men read such books. When I said they were mine, this man was gobsmacked! I was introduced to several unsuitable men including a brick-layer and a store man. They just weren't my cup of tea. And when you meet really odd people, you do it once and don't repeat the exercise.

'On the last day of the holiday, Joan asked me if I thought I might see Ken again. I told her I didn't know. When he rang, he told me that although we'd only been home for a few hours, he'd already told his daughter about our meeting. At that stage, I hadn't told anyone at all. I think it helped that Ken was from the north of England too. In fact, we only lived twenty minutes apart. Had he lived in the South, it might have been too difficult to go on seeing one another. Another plus is that we are on the same academic level. He worked as a civil engineer before his retirement. At our age, when you meet someone who is at a similar financial level, that too makes life so much easier.'

Ken and Angela moved in together in the April following their holiday. Ken's two daughters and sister were all delighted. 'I don't have any children, so my holiday in Tenerife led not only to a marriage but also gave me an adopted, albeit grown-up family,' Angela says. She advises anyone thinking of going on a singles holiday: 'Do choose beginners events where you are likely to meet people at the same social level as yourself before you commit to a longer holiday. But I tell all my single friends to go on Solo's holidays if they're in need of a rest. There's no knowing where they may lead.'

The mixed bag

Twelve years ago, the mature singles holiday scene was in its infancy. Today, not only are there travel agencies like Solo's offering a variety of holidays from short breaks in Britain to exotic jaunts to faraway places with groups of other, similarly aged and similarly minded people, but there are enormous crossovers between many of the different kinds of singles groups in the market place. Companies that started dinner-dating clubs now organise weekend breaks, with trips to places such as the Lake District, or gourmet meals aboard the Orient Express. Entrepreneurs have sussed the enormous need and gaping hole in the market and are filling it with the things that middle-aged couples have always enjoyed, but which have previously been unattainable to all but the bravest of mature singles. Singles social clubs such as Nexus (which we discussed in the last chapter) and ClubSix, which we mentioned earlier in this chapter, arrange interest weekends and holidays, chosen specifically to attract the silver market. The greatest thing about these ventures is that if you choose a trip that interests you, and one that also fits your pocket, the likelihood is that you know before you start that you will have interests in common with your travelling companions. You could spend a weekend in Torquay visiting the Eden project; spend Christmas in Beaconsfield; take a city weekend break in Barcelona or spend fourteen days in Mauritius, reassured before you leave home that not only will you be visiting a place you've yearned to see, but that you will be doing it in the company of other people in your own age group.

Sandra Menoni started her business, Initial Approach, some ten years ago. Initial Approach, based in Dunblane in Scotland, is a mixture of introduction service, events organisation and singles travel agency. It offers the opportunity to meet people through dinner dating, as described earlier in this chapter, dances, outdoor adventure days, 4×4 road driving, hill walking, one-day trips abroad to exciting locations such as Vienna and Rome, and week-long holidays to destinations such as Florida or Rhodes. Members range in age between twenty-one and eighty and the 'occasions', as they are known, are sold on a first-come, first-served basis. There are different levels of membership as well as international links, although most of Initial Approach's members are based in Scotland. You can find them at 4 Beech Road, Dunblane FK15 OLA (telephone 01786 825777), or look at their website www.initial-approach.co.uk to get a taste for the variety of events on offer.

It really is only possible to offer a small sample of all the goodies out there, waiting to be enjoyed by mid-life single people just like you. If you want to enjoy them, you first have to try a few, find the one that suits you best, and then stop procrastinating and *do* it.

5

The Internet

Recently, I went to a wonderful wedding. I unashamedly wept my way through two packets of Kleenex as the bride, one of my closest friends (who looked stunning in her beautiful pale pink bridal gown, delicately embroidered with fine grey stitching), walked down the aisle on the arm of her brother-in-law. It was hard to believe that this was the same lady who, less than a year before, had been a very lonely widow in her early fifties, convinced she'd never live a 'normal' partnered life again.

After more than twelve years alone and some pretty terrible dating experiences, she had vowed she was giving up on dating because she was never going to meet her own Mr Right. But here she was, standing beside her groom beneath the wedding canopy. That they are soulmates is an old-fashioned and rather mushy sentiment, perhaps, but this particular search for a companion had anything but a mushy, old-fashioned, sentimental beginning: they met on the Internet. Their personal Cupid was datingdirect.com.

A 2001 survey showed that more than three hundred thousand British people were cyber dating. By November 2002, Britain's largest dating site, uDate had more than 670,000 members in the UK – but that's small fry compared with the 3,000,000 who regularly surf Internet dating sites in the USA. By September 2002, uDate were claiming an astonishing 13,000,000 members globally. About 30 per cent of them were aged over forty – 60 per cent male, and 40 per cent female, across all age groups. So women are in the *minority* for once.

Mature men may be just as nervous as women about re-entering the dating arena after years in a monogamous relationship. Research has shown that they find Internet dating the ideal medium to meet women in their own age range. 'Our older male subscribers tell us that online dating helps them to meet a wide variety of new female friends quickly and without embarrassment,' says Toby Rowland, uDate's Vice President, Global Communication. 'Mature men are generally nervous about re-entering the dating arena and unsure of how to do it. They will be busy with careers, have children from previous marriages, or have other defining personal circumstances. They can check whether a new woman might be compatible by looking at such things as marriage status, children, smoking habits and so on, even before they start talking.'

The beauty of Internet dating is that you can meet people at *any* time convenient to you, even in the middle of the night. It's a perfect platform for busy professional people, whose working life starts early and ends late, to meet others.

Peter explains:

'After my divorce, I was determined not to be alone. Life is too short. With a busy lifestyle, I didn't have much time to go looking for suitable women, and after years in a monogamous relationship, I had no idea where to start. Internet dating offered me the perfect choice. I looked for someone on the Dating Direct website (www.dating direct.com). I didn't want a smoker or someone with six children, but I did hope to meet a Jewish lady under the age of fifty-five and marked the profiles of two or three women I thought attractive, for future contact. Miriam was among them.

'What I didn't realise at the time, was that each lady then got an automatic email saying that someone was interested in them. So I was most surprised when Miriam sent me an email four hours later suggesting that we correspond. She had registered with the site months earlier and then forgotten all about it. And she'd been so surprised to receive notification of my interest that she'd sent an email straight back. I liked the sound of her so much that when the other women contacted me, I sent emails straight back saying thanks very much but I think I've found the woman I'm going to marry! Miriam didn't know that at the time. We started emailing one another, then chatting on the phone, and I discovered she didn't live too far away from my home in north London, so we then arranged to meet for a meal. We got on so brilliantly that ten weeks later we went on holiday to Prague together and, as they say, the rest is history. I proposed. She accepted. And I couldn't have found a lovelier or more caring wife, beautiful not only on the outside but on the inside too.'

Peter and Miriam had discovered the first golden rule of cyber dating: You are far more likely to be successful in your quest to find the missing piece in your life-jigsaw if you target the profile of someone with whom you have at least one thing in common. Don't concentrate *only* on sites dedicated to older daters. Look for religious, hobby or interest groups. Peter and Miriam were also both extremely lucky. They told the truth about who they were, what their marital situation was and what they were looking for. Not everyone is so fortunate, or so honest.

Cyber dating could be the answer to finding the partner you've been searching for. Hundreds of people of all ages have found new lifetime partners and real happiness, thanks to the Internet. But *don't* rely on it totally, utterly and completely. There are dangers and pitfalls.

Ask yourself:

- Are you adventurous and willing to take a gamble?
- How honest are you – and how honest are you prepared to be?
- If you find a potential date on the Internet, could you tell a close friend?
- How intuitive are you?
- How gullible are you?
- How easily are you hurt?
- What do you expect to gain from Internet dating?

Pros of Internet dating

There can be enormous advantages to seeking a partner on the Internet.

- You can go online and surf through the dating sites at any time of the day or night that suits you.
- You can get to know someone by 'chatting' to them at length on screen without ever revealing your true identity or precise whereabouts (probably a far safer bet for women than meeting up with a strange man in a bar).
- You can take your time and go at your own pace. There's no rush.
- The basic facts of your current lifestyle – such as whether you are single, widowed or divorced, have children, grandchildren and/or pets are revealed up-front. There are no nasty surprises.
- You can meet a compatible partner from anywhere in the world.

The disadvantages of Internet dating

When online, be cautious about the information you may be presenting. Beware of posting personal details on a bulletin board or chat room, or being too trusting of people that you may meet in these environments. Divulging your email address may lead to an influx of undesired messages (spam). Some sites use a small piece of code known as a cookie, which can be used to track your progress through the site. Less desirable sites may abuse this facility, which may make you more vulnerable to receiving unwanted messages. You can protect against this by altering the settings in your browser software to 'deny cookies'.

- You may chat to someone who you then decide you don't want to talk any more, but who then has a note of your email address and becomes a pest. Before you start instant messaging a stranger, check out that your chosen site has a 'blocking' device to prevent this kind of nuisance.
- You may decide to meet someone who sounds perfect on paper, but when you do finally meet in real life, you know instantly that the 'chemistry' for a loving relationship is lacking. Meet someone face to face and you generally know whether or not you like the look of that person within a few minutes.
- People can lie about their details (and can even post photographs of others) and you have no means of checking them out. Recently, a man who described himself as a Pierce Brosnan look-alike on an Internet site actually scanned in a picture of – Pierce Brosnan!
- It can be time-wasting. It takes longer to chat online to someone than to talk in real time. You may spend weeks online and never meet anyone you feel you could form a compatible relationship with, which can be very dispiriting.

If you are chatting online to a stranger, *never* make lude or suggestive remarks, even as a joke. They won't be seen as flirty or funny. Certainly, you won't be demonstrating that g.s.o.h. and worse, you could be permanently banned from the site by a vigilant moderator.

WARNING! BE CAREFUL

This is not just a vague warning. It's a vital matter of personal safety. When you start chatting to strangers on the Internet, you have no idea who you are talking to, whether it be in a chat room or on a one-to-one 'whispering' basis on a dating site.

To go on a date with someone you've met on the Internet, you do need to be adventurous and brave. It takes as much courage to start 'chatting' blind on the Internet as it does to walk into a room full of strangers alone for the first time. Probably more, because you can't see who it is you are speaking to. *You need to be super-cautious.*

Rules for cyber dating security

When you go looking for friends on the Internet, you will meet people you would never otherwise be in touch with – and this applies whatever age you are. But it's as well to bear a few simple rules in mind for security as well as for comfort:

1. Women should ring men rather than the other way round, and always withhold their telephone number before making the call.

2. Women responding to cyber adverts online should *never* give out their real name, address, workplace or phone number. They should only give out their mobile number – but insist on taking a man's land-line phone number. If you

are told only to call at certain times, drop the relationship before it starts. He's almost certainly hiding a wife.

3. Try to find out something about a man before you meet him. This may involve no more than checking his address on the electoral role by going to the local council in the area in which he lives or via www.192.com (in the UK). It's really worth the small subscription.

4. If possible, find someone you know who knows him.

5. After an initial meeting online, do chat via instant messaging before you exchange phone numbers.

6. Do have several phone conversations before you decide to meet.

7. Always arrange to meet in a public place – and tell someone where you are going and what time you intend to be home.

8. Once you've decided to meet, do it. Don't put it off. If you do, you are likely to fantasise and build your cyber-date into a super hero or heroine and you'll fall flat when it comes to the date.

9. Arrange to meet for a coffee or a drink initially. If you arrange an expensive meal and it all goes pear-shaped, you'll be left feeling not only flat but very angry.

10. *Be honest* when you're Internet dating – but not too honest. You must be careful not to reveal too much about yourself or your personal situation to total strangers via a medium that can easily be intercepted.

• Don't get into discussions about finance or property, or discuss what you own or earn – either online or by any other way.

• Do take a close friend into your confidence and explain what you are doing and why. You might even ask someone close to accompany you 'invisibly' on your date and to hover in the background of the restaurant, bar or café when you date an Internet introduction for the first time. Then you know you have a safety valve.

• If you don't have a safety valve, don't get involved with

Internet friendships at any deep level. Remember, you don't know who you're getting involved with. If you are an intuitive person, you may be able to 'feel' you're OK – but even intuition can sometimes fail you.

If you date on the Internet, be prepared for rejection. You may start chatting to someone who sounds wonderful, but when you see their picture, or they see yours, the attraction may not be as powerful as you had hoped it might be. You may even meet them, find them as utterly wonderful as they portrayed themselves to be, only to discover that you've been 'conned'.

Hoaxers

Hoaxers are evil. They're cruel. They get their kicks from causing pain to vulnerable people. You are vulnerable. And sadly, there are an awful lot of hoaxers about on the Internet. They may tell you they're widowers or divorcees when they're not. They may claim to be childless and have a dozen children. Shielded by the anonymity of their PC screen, they can become single, unfettered by offspring, and as rich, free and well-travelled as they like. The picture they post of themselves can be a picture of anyone, they haven't produced a signed affidavit swearing that it really is them. So when you start chatting, keep to the screen for a while and progress very slowly, by way of instant messaging, before you even think of parting with a phone number.

Don't take for gospel everything you are told. Members of one very well-regulated Internet chat room for over-fifties based in Australia became friendly with a gentleman who gave himself the nickname of Dearchap. After a few weeks of going into the chat room, he suddenly disappeared. When he returned, he was full of woe. He told his new chat-room friends that his wife had been seriously injured in a car accident and was in a coma. Everyone, including the rooms' 'monitors', believed him.

The story was so compelling. She was at death's door. Linda, one of those who got emotionally caught up in what later proved to be an enormous scam, says: 'Every time we met Dearchap, he was apparently sobbing. His lovely wife was virtually a "goner". He needed money. And, of course, we all promised to make donations to help him and his handicapped son. But it went on, and on, and on. The monitor became suspicious and traced this person. It forwarded to a private address. It was a great moneymaking scam, a total wind-up. The money was being sent to a post office box number.'

If you visit a chat room, follow a few simple rules:

- Do it because you want to make friends.
- Don't reveal any personal details until you are absolutely certain of the identity of your correspondent.
- Don't give out your real name or telephone number in an open chat area.

Sandy's story

Sandy was widowed at the age of fifty. After her husband's death, she bought a computer. She took classes to update her skills and then, to fill lonely evenings, she found a whole new world of Internet friends through a chat room run by her Internet Service Provider (ISP), and had great fun chatting to people in her own age group from all over the world without going outside her front door. Then, out of the blue, she received an email from someone she had never heard of. Later, she discovered that he'd found and targeted her through the profile she'd posted online, which showed she was widowed, in her fifties, fond of classical music and opera and so on. But after many lonely years, Sandy was not in the least suspicious of her new friendship which seemed to blossom so warmly:

'We started chatting online and he sounded really charming. He appeared to like the things I liked. When I told him Chopin was one of my favourite composers, I was delighted to find he said he was one of his too! I didn't realise that whenever we "chatted" I was offering him clues and he was simply picking up on them. He told me he was an American (true) living near Cambridge (also true) and just working in the UK for six months (a complete lie). He said he was widowed (another lie). I told him what a coincidence that was: I lived near Cambridge, and I was widowed, too. He told me he was fifty-nine (later I discovered he was actually sixty-five). We arranged to meet. "Al" was very good-looking. We enjoyed two or three meals together. Then I got a phone call to say that his brother had died and he'd had to fly back to the States. He would be back at the weekend. He was. He came to see me at home. He met my daughter, my GP, and a neighbour. They all thought he was charming and they were all pleased for me. I felt as though I had woken up after a long sleep. Suddenly, I had something to live for again. It didn't dawn on me that by this time, he not only knew where I lived, but he'd also been able to assess my financial situation.

'He told me he was travelling backwards and forwards to the States on business. I had no reason to disbelieve him. And then it all went quiet. I didn't hear anything from him for ages. Then, to my horror, I received an email from someone calling themselves Jody, claiming to be Al's son. He told me his father had been taken ill and was in hospital. He had been diagnosed with bowel cancer. I was totally distraught. I had lost my husband four years earlier. Now I was in danger of losing someone else I cared for. When he "got home" we messaged one another for a couple of months. We spoke on the phone, and he sounded terribly ill and gave me all the gory details. I didn't see him again. Then his "son" rang to tell me he had "died". I was gutted.

'His "son" kept in touch. He said he'd be "over" in the autumn and would come and see me. He even offered me a job, helping to clear up "Al's" business affairs in the USA and in Europe. That offered the prospect of travel and it sounded like a good deal to me.'

It was around this time that Sandy received a message from another member of the chat room community. He was a widower, and he telephoned her at 11 p.m. one night. He told her he had just been talking to another woman who had been widowed twenty years previously. She had had a similar experience with an American and he, too, had apparently died. He suggested that the two women needed to speak as a matter of urgency. 'I called her there and then,' Sandy says, 'and we were on the phone and Internet for hours, exchanging information about "our" men. When we exchanged photos, we realised that it was the same man! He had done to her exactly what he had done to me, but one month previously.'

A freelance reporter, Alison Jack, who worked for Sky News had become involved and started an investigation. 'Al's' story proved a pack of lies. He was an American living with his English wife on a permanent caravan site in a retirement park near Cambridge. His whole story was a fabrication. He was his 'son' as well as himself. There was no business. He was very much alive. He was bored. Sandy and the other duped woman reported the matter to the police, but they were unable to act, although on a practical level he had practised deception, and Sandy and her friend were not the only vulnerable widows he had targeted. More than a dozen other women had fallen victim to his story. He'd found out about their widowed status via their profiles posted online. He admitted to Alison Jack that he only targeted widows because they were exceptionally vulnerable and would fall for his story.

Sandy searched the Internet for help and discovered www.wiredsafety.org. This is an international organisation which has been set up to monitor Internet abuse, particularly where vulnerable women and children are concerned. Originally set up as Wiredpatrol, it was started by American Parry Aftab to monitor safety in cyberspace, and acts as a guardian, regulating sites which may prey on children and vulnerable adults as well as keeping the media informed of Internet abuse of any kind, including the kind of stalking Sandy and other women have innocently encountered. Wired Safety are the experts on international safety and law and have become an international organisation with branches worldwide, including the UK, where those who have become victims of cyber crime can receive expert counselling and advice. *If you fall prey to an Internet hoaxer, contact the British branch of Wired Safety.*

The upside of Internet dating

I've spelled out the downside of Internet dating, but as you saw at the beginning of this chapter, there can be a very positive side to it too. If you're searching the Internet for love, look in places where you have at least one thing other than age in common with your fellow surfers.

General interest chat rooms

If you have a strong religious conviction, put the relevant religion or hobby and the word 'dating' into your favourite search engine, such as www.google.co.uk, or www.lycos.com, and hopefully it will lead you to a site that suits you. To give you a helping hand, The Christian Connection is at: www.christianconnection.co.uk. This is a great site with message boards which allow you to interact with other people on an enormous variety of issues, and to get to know them before you even start the matching process. You can sign up to Christian Connection for a free ten-day trial period. This will enable you to create a profile, match yourself with other members, and send and receive mail. An additional plus is the ability to record and listen to voice messages. Usually voices offer great clues as to what sort of person owns them, whether they are upbeat or flat; whether interesting and attractive to you or of no interest at all. After that, if you wish to stay on the site, a small subscription fee will be payable. It will cost you £17.50 for a single month and £79.50 (the equivalent of £6.63 a month) if you take out a one-year membership.

Jewish singles will find a whole myriad of both men and women aged from forty upwards on www.totallyjewish.com. Registration on the dating channel is free and offers full access to the site. There are chat rooms too, where once again you can 'chat' online in real time and get to know other people – not all of them singles looking for partners, but you never know who knows someone who knows someone!

One of the biggest problems with the Internet is that it is worldwide. There are no geographical limitations as there may be with dating agencies. When you're online, you will need to give others an approximation of your geographical location so that if and when you do meet, neither of you has to travel too far – and if anything further develops, you won't have to worry too much about uprooting and leaving your family behind.

Almost every hobby has its own chat room. If you find an interest- or age-sensitive chat room, you may make a whole host of new friends, and that might well include a future partner. There are websites for dedicated hikers, gardeners, bridge and chess fiends, and so on. You will find special interest sites all over the Internet. For example, type 'gardening chat' into a search engine such as Google and you will come up with a dozen sites such as www.maigold.co.uk/chat.htm with a chat room open twenty-four hours a day. Committed Christians might try www.christianchat.ca which has a dedicated chat room for the thirty-five-plus age group. There are dozens of chat sites aimed at seniors with or without special interests that you may find through www.agematters.org/senior_chat_rooms.htm. As I've already said, there's vibrant online chat to be had at www.50connect.co.uk. Those who are mad about horses, crazy about cats, or who go dotty over dogs could find like minds to chat to at www.animalforum.com/chat.htm.

Indeed, the key, once again, is to make friends with people of both sexes. Inevitably, once you've established common ground, you will undoubtedly get to talk just as you might talk to any friend with similar interests any time, anywhere. You will follow up with phone calls and who knows where that might lead.

Carole and Graham

Carole had visited a number of overseas chat rooms but found them distant and the chat rather silly, pointless and occasionally offensive. She was delighted to discover a website for the over-forties based in England which had formed a Web 'community' and had a dedicated chat room. It offered her the chance to make friends with other 'members' of both sexes in her own age group. Suddenly, at a time when her personal life was in turmoil and she felt vulnerable and lonely, she had found a whole group of other people in her age band, many of them in the same emotional boat. Instead of feeling isolated, she belonged here. Carole loved it and the 'community' became a very real force in her life: 'I used to visit the chat room attached to the site a couple of nights a week, for company. Gradually, over a period of a couple of months, I got to know people in the room. Everyone was very friendly. No one used bad language and most of us, both men and women, were there for the same reason. Graham often went in there too and we chatted as part of a general crowd.'

The two remained no more than two members of a very large chat-room circle for months. After filing a petition for divorce, Carole involved herself even more in the website and became a forum leader in return for payment of her Internet connection charges. The website instituted a Rogues Gallery. Now she and her fellow chat-room pals could see what their new friends looked like. When she was offered a part-time paid role within her 'community', she jumped at the chance. 'It became an important part of my life,' she says. 'It was a great way of keeping myself amused. People began to want to meet up, so I offered to organise a meeting for everyone in Nottingham and about ten people turned up.'

The social was so successful that Carole, with the backing of the website, arranged another social get-together for members and this time around twenty members turned up in Harrogate.

'Graham had been away when the arrangements were made for the Harrogate get-together. He wanted to come, so he asked me in the chat room whether I minded if we spoke on the phone, rather than boring everyone else by repeating what they already knew. The first time we spoke, we chatted and chatted and chatted. After that, we began to phone one another very regularly. He had never been married, although he told me he had a son from a long-term relationship which had ended years before.'

The couple met for the first time as part of a group in a hotel. Carole says:

'We were both well aware of the dangers any meeting on the Internet can throw up. That first weekend, we talked and we laughed and we went for a walk, but most of the time, we were in company. I felt very reassured about that. I had thought he was a special person the minute I met him, but I was in no position to say anything at that stage. I had no idea how he was feeling and I was scared I might be rejected. He told me later that he was feeling exactly the same way about me. It is no easier when you are fifty than when you are twenty. In fact, if anything, it's harder.'

Despite the initial attraction, it was several months before Carole and Graham did meet privately, and many months more before they decided to move in together. They married in Las Vegas earlier this year. The Internet site through which they met suffered the fate of so many other websites in the early part of the twenty-first century. But Carole and Graham's relationship seems set for a longer, happier and more enduring ending.

Dating sites

There are literally thousands of dating websites based all over the world on the Internet, including dozens which claim to concern themselves only with more mature people. Generally, they're a good bet, especially for women who are finding it hard to meet men of a similar age by conventional methods.

'Acquaintances', which advertise themselves as a website for the more mature person, are one such (you will find them at www.acquaintances.co.uk.). Another site, www.loveandfriends.com, also fields a fair selection of older men as well as women. This is a two-level service offering free information on possible partners and charging an additional £10 a month for wider access to the site, allowing you access to thirty extra features including Matchbot who will email you when someone matching your description registers on the site. British based uDate (you will find them at www.udate.com) is a global website offering a dedicated Internet dating facility for people of all ages, many of them in the forty-plus age range. They charge members £16.95 a month for unlimited access, which includes computer-generated matching online, so that you are offered partners whose profiles may fit with your own requirements.

Before you get too involved, or part with any money, do check out what you get for your 'joining fee'. If you like the look of someone you see on www.udate.com for example, an international site with a vast database, the extra fee you pay allows you to 'whisper' – that is, have a private conversation using a dedicated immediate messaging service, where only the two of you can see what you are saying. There are no limits on how many people you can engage in cyber-relationship with. The only constraint is time. If you don't use up your month's worth, you can't carry it over. However, it's a brilliant idea because it gives both of you the chance to get to know one another *before* exchanging any personal details at all, such as phone numbers. However, before you start filling in Internet forms, try to check as far as you can that your email address won't be given to any third parties, who may target your inbox with rubbish. It's happened to me.

How should you describe yourself?

The formula for self-description on a dating site is quite different from that you would use in a newspaper lonely-hearts ad. For a start, you have more room to play with. Use it wisely. Anything viewed on a computer screen, in a light that is often tiring on the eyes, needs to be informative and snappy. It needs to hold the interest of the reader and tease them into wanting to know more. Most people will download a profile that really interests them. Keep it slick – and keep it clean!

A forty-nine-year-old gentleman posted the following on loveandfriends.com:

Warm, considerate and supportive

I am very sociable, have some very close friends who have been there for me, and I for them, in good and hard times. I have many and varied interests, and am always curious to learn more. I love Art and Art History, have studied it, collect Art books, and visit exhibitions. I go to the theatre, cinema, modern ballet and concerts, mostly classical. I love music and hunting for records – classical, blues, jazz and pop. We (I have two dogs) go out a lot. Walking with friends, country houses, exploring the countryside. I have been lucky and have travelled the world, but there is still so much to see. I prefer travel holidays to, for example, the un-known parts of Italy, but also go to Spain each year just to relax. In sport, I watch football, tennis and motor racing, and play badminton, tennis and golf for enjoyment. People describe me as a kind, creative, and interesting person who gives a lot. I have also run four businesses, so can manage affairs and take difficult decisions if needed. I am looking for a soulmate to love and care for, someone with the same curiosity to explore the riches this life can bring. A wicked sense of humour would be nice, we all need to see the funny side of life.

Personality
Affectionate, adventurous, ambitious, aware, caring, considerate, creative, friendly.

This is a full and very revealing profile. In the space of a couple of hundred words, this gentleman reveals that he is financially comfortable and enjoys a cultured and active life. He has a wide circle of friends, likes animals, and enjoys exercise, particularly walking and adventurous travel. But there's one tiny giveaway. He wants a woman 'to love and care for'. So how might a lady respond? And should those independent spirits who want love but prefer to control their own lives bother to apply?

In her reply, for example, an independent lady might say: 'I live in Gloucestershire (keep the area very general) and love walking, horses and country pursuits. My German Shepherd helps keep me fit with her demands for invigorating walks. I enjoy visiting Art galleries too. My last trip abroad was to see the treasures of Florence. I'm planning a trip to New York because I've never been to the Met. After several years alone, I'm totally independent and enjoy life that way, but I too hope to find someone to love.'

At this stage, keep your responses to email addresses only.

And another happy ending

Twice married and twice divorced, David met Alex, forty-five, his current partner of two years, through uDate.co.uk. 'I had been living and working in the USA for ten years,' he explains. 'When I got back to the UK, most of my old friends were married people, or divorced women with children who were looking for love. What I was looking for was a non-committed relationship, and if it led to more, that would be fine.'

He says he found the whole concept of chatting online very revealing. The reason is that when you are forced to think and then write quickly, there's less time to give a considered response. David reckons he had between thirty and forty real-time dates through uDate over a three-month period. He says he interacted with dozens more. Sometimes he spent an hour or two online. On other occasions, he took his laptop to bed in place of a book, in order to surf for five minutes before going to sleep!

David maintains that joining a regular dating agency was of no help to him in his particular situation. 'The problem is that they're expensive, and if a woman has joined such an agency, then she's looking for commitment,' he says. He felt that what he calls 'analogue' meetings, meeting women through friends of friends or in bars or clubs, are equally unsatisfactory. 'I might spend five minutes with them, feel the chemistry was right, but when the novelty wore off four or five months down the line, I would discover we had nothing further in common,' he says.

'If you break the process of dating down, you can see that you stand more chance of finding something in common with someone through the Internet than you will meeting 'cold' in a club or bar. If you use online dating, you know before you chat to a woman what paper she reads. You can gauge her politics. You can discover her interests and see how they fit in with yours. By the time you reach middle age, you are a little more realistic about what makes a relationship work and what doesn't. You may want to find someone who will help you grow in areas where you would like to grow as well as blend into those places where blending is important. I knew I wanted to find a woman who was more academic and artistic than I am and who would stretch me.'

David and Alex met face-to-face just a short while after meeting online, and discovered a physical, mental and emotional attraction immediately. They had thought about having children together, but can't because Alex is now post-menopausal. They have agreed to limit their interest in children to their young nephews and nieces. 'I think using Internet dating to create an opportunity is a great thing,' David says. 'And I've proved it.'

Behind the websites

One of the major problems with websites is that they can feel such impersonal places. Often, the only contact with 'real' people you have may be through an email with the organisers. Yet, before you commit to joining up and parting with cash, it may be worth doing a little research into people to whom you are entrusting some very personal information. Do check out who is running a site, where are they based, and can you get hold of a real, live human being on the end of a phone if you need to.

Most Internet sites for so-called 'silver surfers', such as www.50connect.co.uk, are run by reputable businessmen and women. Phil Collins and Lynda Hamilton, who started 50connect in Australia and brought it to its Windsor base in Berkshire, may not be in the demographic themselves, but they have a keen understanding of what mature people want from a website, and they saw the potential for growth in the market. Although there is no specific dating site on 50connect, there is a busy love-and-romance message board.

Although they do offer a service to younger people, www.cybersuitors.com is run by Caroline Chamberlain and Jon Cousins, both in their forties, with 'silver surfers' very much in mind. As with so many other interest fields, many dating websites are born out of a personal need. Where Cyber Suitors are concerned, both its founders have had personal experience of searching for suitable partners unsuccessfully in mid-life.

Interestingly, although they've been running their site for some time, neither Chamberlain nor Cousins has yet met their own match through the Internet, or any other medium.

Chamberlain explains:

'We were both older and neither of us had been in a position to go out and meet a partner because of our work patterns and lifestyle. I did put an ad in *The Times* once, because I didn't like replying to other people's ads, and although I got a good response, I decided I didn't like doing that either. I found it embarrassing to go out with someone I knew nothing about. Then Jon, who is forty-six and had been working in a US-based advertising agency, discovered Internet dating. But just as with dating and introduction agencies, time and again we heard stories of people being swept off their feet in a tide of passion, then being brought down to earth with a jolt when they discovered that there was something about their date which meant a relationship was unlikely to work. Perhaps one wanted children and the other didn't. Or one was a smoker and the other couldn't abide it.'

In order to add to the authority of their site, Chamberlain and Cousins have employed the services of eminent psychologist Dr Glenn Wilson, Reader in Personality at the University of London's Faculty of Psychiatry and a world authority on the science of attraction. Years ago, Dr Wilson had devised a romantic compatibility test for one of the very first home computer programmes. Chamberlain and Cousins asked him to design a psychometric compatibility test for their new Internet site. The Compatibility Quotion – or CQ test as it is known – is the result. Chamberlain claims it has been successfully tested on groups of strangers and found to be uncannily accurate:

'For too long, matchmaking has been based on a person (or a computer) pairing up gentlemen who prefer blondes with women who are blondes. It goes a long way to explaining why the whole dating agency scene (both on- and off-line) is such a hit-and-miss experience. We charge $29 – that's around £21 a month – for people to join our site and take the CQ test. Thanks to the test, we are able to assess whether someone will be long-term compatible with someone else. And that's what makes us so much more suitable for older people. Someone of twenty-one is looking for a date for next week. But if you are forty-five years old and sitting at home and have children, you are far more likely to be looking for a serious long-term relationship – and this is the sort of relationship we are trying to put together. We weed out people who are not likely to get on – even if initially they fancy one another physically, they don't think in the same way. And people are far more likely to answer a questionnaire honestly when they pay money upfront and take a test of this kind.'

The Internet can work for mid-life daters as much as for the younger set. And although 'the age thing' is often a major problem in life, there appear to be a huge surplus of over-forty males advertising themselves as looking for love with over-forty ladies in cyberspace. You could, like Miriam and Peter, meet the love of your life. Or it could all end in tears. But BE CAREFUL.

6

Media dating

If you're an extrovert by nature, there's another avenue you might explore in your quest for love. Newspapers, magazines and TV programmes are always looking for suitable candidates to go dating publicly. People of all ages are welcome, and here is one area where the over-forties are often in special demand. Applying to take part in *Blind Date* or *Would Like to Meet* is not as daunting as it sounds, and although the odds may appear to be stacked against you being chosen, if you can prove you have 'chutzpah', it shouldn't be too difficult to persuade the producers or journalists that you're just the person they've been waiting for to have on their programme. Or you might choose to film your profile to be broadcast on The Dating Channel on digital TV.

However, if you decide to embark on a mission to go public on dating, there are two vital things to remember:

1   You must be prepared to face scrutiny by the newspaper journalists or programme presenters.
2   You must be willing for your most private, annoying habits and most inane lifestyle facts to be revealed to an audience of possibly millions.

I have to put my hand on my heart and admit that I've never personally considered media dating. This could be because, even though I'm journalist, and everyone thinks I must therefore be an egoist, I am by nature very shy! However, I'm convinced that if you've got the bottle, it really is worth having a go. Listening to people who've done it, I'm convinced that it's fun. It's also entirely free (apart from the cost of a stamp). You have nothing to lose, and whether or not you are selected to appear on the programme, you'll probably enjoy the excitement of the auditions, possibly a make-over, and a chance to see the inside workings of a TV or radio programme. However, there are some TV shows that are unsuitable, because they are aimed at the very young, so you will need to do your homework, watching them and seeing who appears before you head for the 'front line'.

As you will see later in this chapter, some newspaper dating features, such as 'Matchmakers' in the *Daily Mail*, are aimed specifically at the forty-plus age group. And as you're never too old to love, there's no reason why you shouldn't be game for a laugh.

Talent

Before you decide to go media dating, can you put your hand on your heart and own up to the following personality traits? Tick the boxes below and see how you score:

1. Are you a natural born extrovert? Yes ❏   No ❏
2. Are you willing to laugh at yourself in public and have others laugh with you and at you? Yes ❏   No ❏
3. Are you prepared to reveal your personality for perusal by Joe Public? Yes ❏   No ❏
4. Are you the lucky possessor of sheer chutzpah?
   Yes ❏   No ❏

5. Do you have the gift of wit and rapid repartee?
   Yes ❑   No ❑
6. Do you recognise your own failings? Yes ❑   No ❑
7. Are you prepared to be 'sent up' by a celebrity host or hostess? Yes ❑   No ❑
8. Can you show a little humility in public? Yes ❑   No ❑
9. Are you tenacious enough to keep trying, even if you don't succeed the first time? Yes ❑   No ❑
10. Do you believe that you could find the love of your life, despite your age, if only other people recognised your virtues? Yes ❑   No ❑

If you have ticked 'yes' to at least six of the above ten questions, then you're probably exactly the kind of candidate researchers are looking for to help get their show on the air. *Remember, however, that these researchers are looking for candidates who make good viewing, listening or reading. They go for people who are prepared to admit they're a little 'different' and rather more interesting than your average, run-of-the-mill Ms or Mr Brown. You need to look good. You need to feel good. You need to think positively. You do need a massive sense of humour. The whole point is that while your ambition is to find the love of your mid-life, theirs is to improve their sales or up their position in the ratings.*

TV dating

TV dating programmes are compulsive viewing. They attract enormous audiences and huge postbags of people anxious to be featured on the shows. And age is absolutely no bar to appearance. What you need is charisma, personality and sheer, blatant guts.

Lillian was a seventy-one-year-old divorcee when she wrote off to *Blind Date* for a bit of fun. Nine years later, she's happily married to David, the man she met on the programme. He was then a seventy-year-old widower whose wife had died just eighteen months previously. 'I started laughing when I arrived at the studio for the first audition and I'm still laughing,' she says. And so she should be. At the time they met, she lived in Newcastle Upon Tyne. He lived in Devon, in the south-west. Their chances of meeting would have been less than zero without the help of the programme made famous by its celebrity hostess, Cilla Black.

Lillian's first letter of application was a 'cold call'. She'd dated several men in the nine years since her divorce, including a dancing partner she'd had for five years, but she'd turned down several proposals of marriage and vowed she would never tie the knot again. As far as she was concerned, her application to appear on the programme was all a big joke. Something she could do for the sheer fun of it. So, when she opened the letter in response to hers to discover she'd been invited to an interview, she says she nearly fell off her chair from shock. 'We had a brief chat and I was told that I would be recalled if they wanted to take it further,' she says. Three months later, the phone call she never expected came. 'They asked me if I would go to Edinburgh for a second interview. It was quite an experience. I had to stand up and talk about myself for ten minutes.

'There were eleven ladies at the audition that day but I was the oldest. We had a make-believe *Blind Date*. I was number three. The first question from the pretend date, Mike, was: "My young sons say they can't keep up with me because I'm too fast for them. How would you cope?" I replied: "Make sure I kept taking the vitamins. Because anything you can do, I can do better." The next question was: "My boy is learning statistics in school. What do you know about it?" I told them the only statistics I knew anything about were my own vital statistics − 36, 24, 38." At that, Mike, virtually jumped into the air and told me: "If you're telling the truth, Number Three, you have a fantastic figure." I *was* telling the truth. I was and still am quite shapely and slim. When the audition was over, we were all told to go home and forget about it. Three months later I had another phone call asking me if I was still interested in appearing on the programme and I said I was. At this interview, the girl who chatted to me told me I ought to be a "picker". Then she told me to go along to the studio on the 11 October with a suitcase packed ready for my date. I had to prepare twelve questions in advance of the recording and the producers chose the best three. They really do use the picker's questions.'

David applied at his daughter's prompting. She had seen an advert in the local paper for candidates to appear on the programme and suggested he ought to go along. So there he was, sitting as Number Three, waiting for Lillian.

Lillian clearly remembers the questions she asked him – and his rapid responses!

'I told him: "I dress up in a French maid's costume to do a Kissogram turn to raise money for the Church and the British Heart Foundation. I do love dressing up in fancy dress but what outfit would you like me to wear?" David gave me by far and away the best answer. He said: "As a representative of the Post Office, I would like you to wear three first class stamps, strategically placed, which would give me a male (mail) advantage!" My second question was: "I'm very emotional and cry at sad movies. When the lights went up to reveal my sore, red eyes, what would you do to comfort me?" David said: "I could sing you a song. It might cheer you up – or it might make you feel worse." At that, Cilla put her head around the partition and said: "Go on, David. Lillian wants to hear you." So he sang: "Any old iron". For the third question, I said: "Although I'm seventy-one, I love having a go on the swings in the children's playground. What is your favourite playground gadget?" He said his favourite was the Helter-Skelter because we could share the same mat and finish the ride entwined together. But I didn't choose David for his quick answers. I chose him for his quiet voice. I am the noisy one and he's the quiet one in this relationship.'

The couple went to Jersey on their date:

'It was fantastic,' Lillian says. 'We had such a wonderful time. We married at Tiverton Registry Office on 5 February 1994. Cilla Black and her late husband Bobby came along to our wedding reception. It was a wonderful occasion and of course, we went back to the hotel where we'd had our first date, for our honeymoon. I'd encourage anyone to have a go. Of course, you have to bear in mind that they audition a huge number of people for very few places on the show. But as far as David and I are concerned, meeting on *Blind Date* was like winning the lottery. We both found happiness.'

Blind Date, hosted by Cilla Black in Britain for eighteen years until her retirement at the end of the last series, is the longest-running TV dating programme on air and has been copied worldwide. Shows on a dating theme, where the viewer can become a voyeur on a date between two complete strangers, have been proven to attract enormous viewing figures. There are many such media dating opportunities around, if only you know where to find them.

How to find advertisements

If you would rather not 'cold call' such shows, as Lillian did, you might target specific shows by responding to adverts. New programmes in particular advertise for 'subjects' in *Time Out* and *Private Eye*, and you can check out websites such as www.whowantstobeontv.co.uk or www.rdfmedia.com/news. htm where researchers often seek out volunteers to appear on their shows (including dating shows like *Perfect Match*). The former is a website dedicated to those who are serious about appearing on TV game shows of almost every description and every new dating show ever suggested will advertise here for contestants. The rdfmedia site is more of a job site, but sometimes, among the job ads for news presenters and paparazzi photographers, ads appear for people to appear on other cult programmes, including TV dating programmes both in Britain and the USA. Such advertisements can also be found on www.talent-scouts.org.uk/backstagepass.htm. If you see an ad and want to respond, it may cost you £10 to sign up for some (but not all) of these sites, but that's a small price to pay for the chance of fame and possibly a lifetime partner. A recent ad buried on TalentScouts, in among the job ads for press photographers and political journalists, was for candidates living in Southern California to appear on a Reality TV dating game show to be broadcast nationwide across the USA. Age was no bar. Indeed, from the way the advert was worded, 'silver applicants' were warmly welcomed. Of course, by the time you read this, that show will have been filmed and probably aired too. But as the old proverb goes, seek and ye shall find. You email, write, ring or fax a dating show or newspaper dating feature that catches your interest and, if you're lucky enough to be chosen from the hundreds of applicants most of these shows attract every week, you're on your way to a great experience – and maybe the love of your life. More and more TV companies and publications are aiming at the mature dating market. There's obviously plenty of life in us old 'dogs' – and 'bitches' – yet!

Have you got attitude?

There's the world of difference between attitude and arrogance. Attitude is personality-plus. Arrogance is self-love, bordering on rudeness.

If you're considering applying to date on a TV programme such as *Blind Date*, *Would Like to Meet*, *Final Score*, or even a one-off show you see advertised, your first requirement is real attitude. You need to show what a strong and positive personality you are. Shy mortals need not apply. The message you need to put across is: 'I want to meet a mate. I don't mind being seen (and possibly pulled apart) in front of an audience of millions in my quest. I can laugh at myself. I'm a fun person. Choose me to go on your programme or feature in your newspaper, and I'll prove my worth by increasing your viewing figures or sales. PLEASE MATCH ME.'

Warning!

The programme makers, journalists, magazines and newspapers who sponsor these programmes may seem like fairy godmothers/fathers. But make no mistake about it, their 'good deed' in researching likely partners for would-be lovers, dressing them up, paying for them to enjoy lovely meals in top restaurants and possibly treating them to dream holidays comes at a price. The bottom line is that it is the producers' and writers' job to entertain, amuse and excite the rest of us. While the producers, presenters and writers may show their subjects loving, caring consideration, the money they invest in giving people a good time is money invested in making a successful programme or ensuring a riveting read. *Have no illusions. You will be the tool by which they will aim to achieve their high readership or viewing figures. You need to be willing to be an entertainer*. If you're still not deterred, read on.

Identify your 'quarry'

You need to identify the kind of programmes or the sort of features that appeal to you, of course, and the one you believe will offer you the best chance of really getting lucky and being matched with a truly possible date. The only way to do this effectively is to read voraciously and tune in to every single dating programme you hear about. Discern what qualities the contestants share (for example, everyone on *Blind Date* appears to be the possessor of rapid repartee whereas all the *Would Like to Meet* contestants have to learn to cope with quite deep and possibly hurtful criticism in front of the cameras), and then decide where you fit best.

Stand out from the crowd

Having decided on your quarry, write off to the programme-makers or editors. Make sure your letter stands out in a crowd. If you're keen to be noticed, you have to do something about it. The public loves reading about other people's dates, and everyone enjoys the voyeurism of programmes such as *WLTM* where daters are pulled into shape very publicly and then sent off to learn how to use their skills.

How to get noticed

- Go to the local quick print shop and order some unusual notepaper. Or get to work on your computer and design something eye-catching. Maybe choose a bright colour such as red with your address printed in solid black. Or something with a logo that screams something about your personality or your sense of humour.
- Write a cheeky letter. It might be along the lines of: 'I've been watching your programme and I'd love to come on the show. And you really do need me, because I've noticed you haven't had any grannies or grandads on in a while. Don't you know that we can be great material? All we need is the chance.'
- If you're replying to a web-based advert, make sure your communication stands out from the crowd. Create the kind of profile for yourself that makes you sound so irresistible and quirky (media people love quirky) that they can't resist inviting you to a first audition. However, be careful to distinguish between original and off-the-wall. If you go too far, you won't stand a chance.

- Enclose a photograph of yourself. Look your very best. You might wear something outrageous for your 'model' photograph, but don't make it so outrageous that you look scary or overpowering. Show you have style.

The Dating Channel

Digital TV offers all kinds of new opportunities to go dating, whatever your age. The Dating Channel is dedicated to helping people of all ages find partners. 'When the channel was launched, it tended to attract a younger crowd, but we're finding that the older age group are happy to use us, too,' admits Noemi Spanos, one of the channel's coordinators.

The Dating Channel send out crews to film dating events in pubs, clubs and bars all over Great Britain. But for the more introverted who like the idea of making a TV debut but at their own pace, The Dating Channel offers every 'single' of any age the chance of a professionally filmed profile which will then be screened at the company's expense and posted on their website. Applicants call (020 7748 1500), write or visit The Dating Channel's website at www.thedatingchannel.com (you can join in online, too). Punters are invited to attend an hour-long appointment at the channel's London studios where they sit with other hopefuls to relax and enjoy a glass or two of champagne and nibbles before being invited into a small studio for their big moment. Unlike other media dating, there is no make-up or make-over ordeal. Once in the studio, it's a matter of sitting down and responding to the interviewers' questions, some serious, some lighthearted, intended to show off your true personality. Later, the producer's questions are edited out so it looks as though you are simply sitting chatting away to camera. Then you and your mobile number are broadcast to the thousands of viewers who regularly tune in to the channel. Your profile can also be viewed on the Internet. It costs just a small sum to receive a password, allowing you an hour's worth of profile viewing on your computer.

Newspaper matchmaking

Many newspapers and magazines currently run regular dating features. Perhaps one of the most successful is 'Matchmakers' which features in the Monday 'Self' section of the *Daily Mail*, which boasts a readership of over three million.

The section invites readers to write in, enclosing a photograph and answering a number of standard questions. These include details of age, location, star sign, number of children (if any), details of books, films, hobbies and interests, salary bracket, height and ideal holiday. Candidates need to respond to other, rather more offbeat queries too, such as what they consider to be their best – and worst – personality traits, their favourite items of clothing, their most embarrassing moment, and traits they deplore in the opposite sex and their relationship history.

According to Amy Anderson, originator and editor of 'Matchmakers', most of those who respond tend to be over forty, and most are aged between forty and fifty-five. The oldest so far selected was sixty at the time of going to press. Between twenty and thirty people apply to take part in the exercise each week. Every eight weeks, the paper invites a selection of eight would-be daters to travel (all expenses paid) to London, where they are invited into a studio, treated to a make-over and a photo shoot. Readers are then invited to write in and offer to date any of the punters they fancy. The post-bag after such a feature can run to between seven hundred or eight hundred letters. 'We bin about 50 per cent of the applications we receive as unsuitable without even contacting them,' says Amy Anderson. These include men who still live with their mothers, people of both sexes whose mothers write in on their behalf, people who've had multiple marriages and divorces, and those who have relatively low-grade jobs for their age. 'The job status/ salary qualification applies more to men than women because we do take into account that many women go back to work after bringing up a family and take low-paid employment in their efforts to return to the work place.' Sending in a photograph is also part of the deal. Anderson says she excludes anyone who is hideously ugly or obese. Married men looking for 'a bit on the side' are also excluded at source!

'Matchmakers' narrow applicants down further by selecting people in the same geographical area. Researchers then look at the details, trying to match personalities, hobbies and child status. When, finally, Anderson has put together what she hopes is like with like, she and her team invite them to a restaurant, generally chosen by the woman, for dinner at the *Daily Mail's* expense.

When the dates are done, Anderson rings both parties and asks for their reactions to their dining companions. 'I'm appalled at how fussy some middle-aged women are,' she says. 'They are totally unrealistic about what they want in a man. They want a knight in shining armour to come along and change their lives, rather than helping themselves. What astounds me is how people don't look at themselves. Even after they've been divorced once or even twice, they still don't realise that perhaps they are responsible for at least half their own problems. Many middle-aged women are so arrogant; they will write a man off because he doesn't hold a door open at the beginning of an evening. I think the real problem is that both men and women tend to be inflexible by the time they reach their mid-forties.'

If you are planning on applying to join the media dating game or to respond to someone who's given it a go:

1. Appreciate that they are more interesting than they might at first appear. They've had the guts to do it.
2. Don't go along with preconceptions.
3. Accept that however 'normal' it appears, media dating

where cameras may be following you and, later, a journalist or TV presenter may be questioning you, is an alien situation. Allow at least an hour before you start to judge the person you are dating. It takes that long to settle down, relax and forget the circumstances under which you have met. Nerves manifest themselves in many different ways.

4. Don't go along thinking that you must not have a drink in case you disgrace yourself. It's a good thing to loosen up and relax – but don't get carried away in relax mode and get drunk.

5. Don't see your media dating experience as the biggest thing in your life. Many people do and pin all their hopes on their media date, only to have them all fall flat. Look at it philosophically. At the very worst, you will spend an interesting evening with people outside your own circle who you don't know and might never have met any other way. At best, you will get on like a house on fire and see one another again.

7

Making the most of yourself

So, you've got a date. Or you're going to a 'do' where the man or woman of your dreams may just be lurking in wait for you. This could be the first glimpse of what might be the beginning of a whole new relationship – and perhaps a new way of life. You want to like and be liked. You want to impress and be impressed. You want to be seen for the warm, loving, kind and witty person you really are. Yet although you're forty-something, or maybe even fifty- or sixty-something, and you've done this entire meeting, dating, mating bit before, you don't know where to start.

Don't be desperate

You may be lonely, but *never* be desperate to meet a new partner. Desperation has a strong, and often offensive, stench that can act as a powerful deterrent. 'Cool' and relaxed, on the other hand, has a delicate aroma which makes you all the more enticing. Mid-life really can be the best time of your life, if only you let it.

Look at the positives

- You have proved a success in your work.
- You have proved you can live as an independent being. You may have more money in your pocket than ever before – but even if you have had to fight for what you've got, you can stand proud in the knowledge that you have done things for yourself.
- As a parent, you may be enjoying the freedom that having older children brings. The world is your oyster. You can travel. You can take off for adventure weekends at the drop of a hat, leaving the kids to cope with the dog. You can look forward, just a few years hence, to a time when work will be only an option and not a necessity.
- You are empowered with a new freedom, and yet that freedom may itself exaggerate your loneliness. 'I'd go to Peru, or the Canadian Rockies if only I had someone to share it with,' you may say. 'I can't walk on the Great Wall of China because I'm alone and it's no fun at all when there's no-one to share it with.' But walk the Great Wall of China you can. You can surf in Sydney or dine on the exquisite delicacies served on the Orient Express. It's just a matter of knowing where to find the adventure you dream of – and possibly through that adventure, a partner in a similar situation who may be delighted at the prospect of finding you.
- Find what you want to do, and you will discover that there's a whole world waiting to be explored; who knows what might happen along the way. By grabbing opportunities that arise in both hands, and insisting that nothing in the world can stop you in your goal to attain what you want, you're halfway there.

Be yourself

The most important thing in your favour is that you have all the benefit of experience and you've lost the artlessness of youth. You may be one of those lucky women who still have the same sexy shape as they had at twenty. Maybe the years and child-bearing have turned the scales against you and these days you're cuddly as well as curvy. If you're a guy, the hair may well be receding and the paunch a little more bulbous than it was in years gone by. But you are what you are. If you start to pretend to be something you're not at this stage, you may find you have to live with a lie for the rest of your life.

It may be that it's a long time since someone told you that they think you're beautiful. That your eyes are the brightest, your conversation the wittiest and most scintillating, your personality the most caring that they've ever come across. Yet it's exactly this kind of sweet-talk that makes us brighter, funnier and more attractive. The more someone flatters us, the better company we will be. The idea of starting from scratch all over again can be quite daunting in mid-life, especially if you're very shy or you've taken a few hard knocks. But remember, you are the person created by your experience. There is no one else quite like you. And whether you're beautifully in shape or chubby, whether you've got a paunch or bunions, whether you are a beautiful person or you need to make the most of your God-given gifts, confidence is attractive. Be confident. You've done it before. You know what you're doing. Believe in yourself.

First impressions

First impressions are vital. Psychologists have proved that we judge people almost instantaneously. Within forty seconds of an encounter, we will decide whether they are attractive, whether we can get on together. We have formed a judgement as to whether or not they are our 'type'; whether we are going to like or dislike them and whether or not we want to see them again – all in the blink of an eye. The initial judgement will be confirmed by our opinions of their speech and body language. So it follows that no matter where you go or what you do to meet a new companion, possibly a lifetime partner, if you give off the wrong vibes, you may deprive yourself of the perfect spouse before you've even introduced yourself.

Many people who've come out of a long-term relationship, and this applies to men as well as women, may have taken a huge ego-knock when a relationship foundered, a marriage ended in divorce, or when they've been widowed. It may be that for years, you've endured classic put-downs from a cruel partner who's criticised you for being too fat, too thin, too boring, too obsessed or too careless with your appearance.

Take a long hard look at yourself. Be honest. What do you see? Make a note of your best features – and your worst. Think back to compliments you have had in the past. Are people always saying what beautiful eyes you have? What glorious hair? What an amazing figure or physique? Take a look in the mirror and examine that bit of yourself that you've been told is most attractive. What can you do to enhance it further? If your true beauty is in long-lashed eyes, or fine clear skin or a glorious mop of hair, why not invest in a beauty session where not only will you be able to relax with a treat such as an aromatherapy massage or a facial, but you can be made up or coiffured by an expert. As they apply the cosmetics, ask what they're doing and why. What colours are they using? When my youngest daughter married, a professional did my make-up for the first time in my life. It was wonderful, but the biggest surprise was in the beautician's choice of colours to suit my skin. I was using the same boring old make-up I'd worn for the past twenty-five years. I hadn't realised that as my hair whitened, the pigmentation of my skin changed too. Changing my eye make-up and opting for a deeper tone of bronze-tinted lipstick took years off my age. The most exciting part of the whole exercise was that this was no one-off. I watched how the beauty therapist worked, and then repeated it for myself (and still do) with very pleasing results.

Mirror, mirror

Try this exercise: look in a full-length mirror. Stand naturally and look hard. No cheating! What do you see?

- If I were meeting me for the first time, would I like what I see?
- Does my hair need a good cut?
- Would a little attention to colour help?
- Does my make-up need modernising?
- Do my nails need attention?
- Do I need to lose or gain a little weight? (Many women in particular who have suffered the trauma of divorce or widowhood lose or gain weight rapidly and begin to look drawn and haggard or bloated.)
- How do I sound when I speak? Is my voice shrill or grating? Can I lower the tone or alter the emphasis of my speech to make it more attractive?

This questionnaire is not intended only for women. Men, too, can ask themselves:

- Do I care for my skin and my hair?
- Do I need to hide behind an old-fashioned beard?
- Are my nails neat and clean?
- Do I polish my shoes?

Both sexes can take a good look at the overall picture they present to the world by studying their wardrobe. Are you stuck in a fashion rut? Are you dressing now in exactly the same style you've always worn?

Whatever your answers, think about how you can improve

yourself and make yourself into the man or woman who will be most desirable person at the party.

General appearance

You want to look modern and stylish, but not look like mutton dressed as lamb. Men may fear that a potential new lady-friend will be 'turned off' by lack of hair or a beer belly, while women, aware that middle-aged and older men have a 'thing' about age, may be so anxious to make themselves look as young and sexy as possible, that they smuggle make-up and clothes out of the house and dress in the loo at the venue, for fear that teenage sons and daughters will mock their efforts at trying to be trendy.

Style consultant Jay Hunt, who has worked as personal shopper to stars such as Jodie Kidd and Emma Forbes in London, New York and Los Angeles, advises punters on the BBC's popular dating show *Would Like to Meet* (where experts offer to re-invent people who want to look their best and act in their most endearing way to attract the love of their dreams). She stresses that after many years of dressing to please a partner, this is the time to dress to please yourself. 'You need to start making your own set of fashion rules and dressing for yourself,' she says. 'You need to dress in a way that makes you feel sexy and confident, and in a way you are comfortable with. You no longer have the safety net of knowing you look the way your partner enjoys seeing you, or perhaps the restrictions imposed on you by dressing to please someone else, but which have, either way, restrained your dress code in the past.'

Hunt advises ladies to get modern but not to attempt to get too trendy for the crucial first date. 'That will often frighten men away,' she says.

Hunt advises forgetting the clothes shops where you've shopped for years and instead, checking out some of the younger, trendier stores:

'Shops such as Karen Millen and Warehouse cater for everyone from eighteen to sixty-eight, especially where separates are concerned. Use your judgement. A pair of hipster pants or a mini-skirt may be the wrong shape or style for your more mature hips, but team a pair of well-fitting trousers with a modern, bright and possibly sparkly top and you'll feel and look bang up to date.

'For a first date, try and wear the sort of outfit you might wear to go out to lunch with a girl-friend. Always dress in a suitable outfit for a venue. That might sound patronisingly obvious, but the mid-life generation do tend to overdress rather than under-dress.'

No! I'm not going to tell you to buy beautiful sexy black undies just in case you fancy the pants off one another on that crucial first date and end up baring more than your souls. (And who says there's no sex over-forty or fifty or sixty?) But undergarments are important, not least because the right control garments, favoured by us slightly rounder mortals who have become cuddly with age (well, that's my excuse!), can do wonders, whereas all-in-ones, long-line bras and high-waisted pantie girdles just half-a-size too small can prove disastrous. The bit that's so wonderfully held in will just pop out somewhere else, on your boobs, your waist, or the top of your thighs. Bits will be escaping all over the place.

Dress for the occasion. If you're going out for spaghetti in an Italian restaurant and you always manage to splash sauce, avoid white or light tops. Wear something dark on top instead. Always be careful to choose a size that fits, because if a garment feels tight, you will fidget all evening, trying to pull it down or up – or you may suddenly feel desperate to loosen a waistband. If it feels too tight, why torture yourself for nothing more than a size in a label? When you're on tenterhooks anyway, being comfortable and feeling sure of your appearance leaves you with one less problem to worry about.

Dress sense

When you're dressing for maximum effect to entice that special man – or to keep him interested:

- Only reveal one small part of yourself. Choose either to show legs or cleavage, or go for backless but not more than one of the three.
- Sheer-look make-up is much more flattering on older skin than wearing both foundation and powder. Forget the old-fashioned methods of testing make-up colours on your wrist. Try some of the make-up counters you've never visited before and ask them to try one or more of their sheer bases on your skin. Then go outside and look at it in your mirror in the daylight. It's no good trying to make a judgement under shop lights. Instead of trying to 'infill' the crow's feet round your eyes with foundation or powder, avoid the whole eye area.
- Blusher can be very ageing. Avoid anything orange or bronze. Any orange or bronze blusher applied as a hard line down the side of the face looks false. Go for the more modern way of applying pale pink blusher in a circular movement on the apples of your cheeks.
- Avoid hard colours on eye-shadow, as well as sparkle, glitter or anything that says iridescent on the label. Such colours only serve to accentuate wrinkles and saggy eyelids. Neutral beiges and browns applied lightly are much more flattering.
- The easiest thing of all to update is lip colour. Forget strong blocks of colour. They are passé. Go for lip-glosses – the ones you can buy that look like a pencil – and go for colours like caramel, toffee or subtle pink. Gloss really flags up an older face and looks sheerer, modern and far prettier.

The biggest mistakes older women can make when they are on a first date are:

- wearing see-through clothes;
- wearing a revealing 'little black dress';
- wearing leopard skin;
- wearing red.

People assume that black suits everyone but it doesn't. Think about wearing black on the lower half of your body, particularly if you are conscious about your hips or stomach. Disguise the bottom half with dark trousers or a dark skirt, and only worry about adding colour on top. Leopard-skin prints make middle-aged women look like barmaids. Black tends to look tarty and hard, and red is a bad idea because men subconsciously read red as 'I'm up for sex tonight.' This includes bright red lipstick and red nail varnish. The 'big age' thing where nails are concerned is that forty-plus ladies often have very long nails. The more modern style is to have them shorter, filed to a square shape and French manicured.

Hair

It's not called your 'crowning glory' for nothing. Well-cared for hair can enhance your looks. Neglect your mop and you will look 'unfinished', no matter how much attention you have paid to the rest of you.

- If you can, splash out on at least one really good, expensive haircut at the best hairdresser in the area. Look on it as an investment. Once hair has been cut to a great shape, it's easier for a less experienced stylist to copy the cut and colour.
- Avoid covering grey hair with a single colour. Two colour tones are far more natural.
- Avoid hair spray at all costs. Older women tend to use it far too much, yet hair that looks as though it can move is much sexier than static hair.
- Hairdressers will always advise you to stay within two colour tones of your natural hair. Go for tortoiseshell highlights in

two or three shades rather than a block of solid colour. Don't go for reddy plum or mahogany tones. They are far too hard. If they're colours you love and you don't want to abandon them, break them up with highlights.

Feet

OK. You may think no one is going to stare at your feet when you're out meeting, or hoping to meet, the perfect companion. But strangely enough, they often do! Seeing a beautifully dressed and carefully polished woman wearing open-toed sandals and sporting yellow, thickened toenails can be distinctly off-putting. If you're going open-toed, with or without tights, invest in a pedicure or at the very least, do paint your toenails.

Scented or smelly?

According to Jay Hunt, most women of all ages have no idea how strong their scent really is. 'A woman will generally shower or bathe before they go out, using a shower gel or scented soap. She may then apply moisturiser with a different scent, rub her hands with handcream which has another bouquet, and then spray herself with her favourite eau-de-toilette or perfume. The combined aromas could knock a man back and sideways as he walks through the door.

Glasses

Unfortunately, when it comes to ageing, you can hide wrinkles, disguise hair colour, buy clothes to flatter your shape, and paint your nails. The one thing both men and women may have to concede as Father Time marches relentlessly forward is the need to wear reading glasses to see a menu. So there you are, sitting at the table with your date. The waiter hands you the menu. I remember my late mother regaling me with the old saying that 'men don't make passes at girls who wear glasses'. If that was your mother's message, then remember it's come from a world gone-by. Imagine you've left your specs on the hall table at home and can't see a single word on the menu at the posh restaurant your lovely date has suggested: 'I'll have what you're having,' you say, to dodge the need to confess that you can't read the menu. 'It sounds good.' And when the boiled beef and mashed potatoes – billed as a classy French dish – appears, you choke on every mouthful and curse vanity and first dates in that order. Sound familiar? According to Hunt, what most women don't realise is that the glasses they so despise can become a flirting tool. You can put your glasses on to study the menu, take them off in a sexy manner to emphasise a point as you look straight into his eyes, you can twiddle them in your fingers as you listen to his riveting conversation, or place them beside your plate. Even those who don't need them might consider them an asset.

Unisex musts

- Make sure your fingernails are clean and well-shaped or manicured. Professional silk-wraps or acrylic can work miracles on very short or bitten nails – even for men. There's nothing 'cissy' about having a professional manicure.
- Ensure your shoes are spotless and well-brushed or shiny depending, of course, on the material.
- Watch your mouth, literally. There's nothing wrong with uneven teeth but they have to be absolutely clean, so if you're planning to start dating again, a visit to the dentist for a scale and polish might be well worth the effort.

Men need style too

According to Jay Hunt, middle-aged men are every bit as vulnerable and in need of a helping hand in the style department as women. 'The biggest mistake middle-aged men make when they start dating again is that they tend to overdress,' she says. 'They think they need to be seen to be making an effort, turn up in a tucked-in shirt and tie and a double-breasted pin-stripe suit for a first date in a pub and think they look like matinee idols. In fact, their formal appearance makes them look staid and dated. What they need to do is relax. They can wear a traditionally cut suit if that is what makes them feel comfortable, but I generally advise that they try a heavy linen or cotton rather than a conventional wool or worsted suit, and buy a shirt cut straight across at the bottom so that it can be left hanging out. A shirt with a U shape at the bottom does need to be tucked in. Leave the neck open; forget the tie. If you've arranged to meet in a wine bar, there's nothing wrong with going along in jeans. Dark denim jeans look smart, and you can't compare them with the Michael Winner/Jeremy Clarkson style faded, bleached look. Dark denim looks great on mature men, especially teamed with a cotton or linen shirt. Go for what are called 'relaxed fit' jeans or wider fit jeans if you are a little wider than you used to be or suffer from a bit of a beer belly. That will balance out your shape – but don't even think of going the seventies flares route. Look at the length at which younger men wear their trousers: they're an inch or two longer than older gentlemen are used to wearing them. Don't be tempted to tuck a shirt into jeans and finish off with a belt.

Men need style tips as much as ladies do. They may not choose to believe it, but as every woman knows, men who try to disguise their age by using 'tricks' such as toupees to hide balding pates or hair-dyes which don't match the colour of their beards can actually add decades to their appearance.

Male dress tips

- It's more flattering to get your hair cut very short than to try dressing it bouffant-style or comb-over style. Bruce Willis has gone for the very short look and he looks great. If you're really bothered by a shortage of hair, why not go for the shaved head look.

- Logos on ties, jokey cuff-links and cartoon-character socks are all no-nos. They do *not* show a good sense of humour.
- Women tend not to like men in jewellery. On a first date, at least, leave the gold chains off!
- Don't be tempted to use too much aftershave. Women don't like it. If you've had a shower and used a good shower gel, that clean, fresh smell is much more appealing.
- If you've got a beard, lose it. A lot of men have had a beard for years and use it as a security blanket. If it hurts to go bare, go for the heavy stubble look which is much more modern, especially when you are going grey. Salt-and-pepper beards are very unappealing.

Jay Hunt offers one other piece of essential advice to men who were brought up in an era when courtesy towards a woman included presenting her with chocolates and flowers: 'Many men take flowers and chocolates on a first date to make themselves appear romantic. It may feel like a chivalrous act, but *Don't*. 'If first impressions appeal, send flowers afterwards as a "Thank you", and tell her how much you'd love to see her again.'

Body language

Of course, it's not all about looks. There are many millions of mature single men and women who dress impeccably, who pay great attention to the detail of their appearance, and who still can't seem to find the perfect mate. So what about body language? Can you walk into a room full of strangers, alone? Many people can't. They will look down, not forwards which can make them look dour. They may huddle with their arms around themselves in self-protective mode rather than relaxing, opening out their bodies and smiling. This is not a criticism, just a truism. If that's the way you're made, you can't change your nature. But you can work on changing the body language signals you emit, so that instead of saying: 'Keep off' you are inviting, and saying: 'I'm just the sort of person you want to meet, even though I'm rather shy, and I'd love the chance to get to know you better.'

- Show a genuine interest in the people you meet. Listen to their questions.
- *Always* be polite. The man you're talking to may well be the last person on the planet you want to date, but the hunk in the corner you really fancy may well be watching you. Perhaps he'll come over when your conversation with Mr or Ms Unsuitable is at an end!

When you haven't dated for years, and are used to being with someone who knows you, your likes, dislikes and history well, the thought of spending hours on a one-to-one basis with a total stranger can be as daunting for men as it is for women. What will you talk about if not your ex, your late partner or your children? How will you explain your politics, your reading habits, your love or hatred of particular films or theatre? When you're starting from point zero, how can you build a relationship from scratch?

Communicating

It would be idiotic to try to suggest subjects for discussion with your date. It's not what you say but the way that you say it, according to Jeremy Milne, another of *Would Like to Meet*'s experts.

Remember that while it's true that you will be embarking on any new relationship with 'baggage', so will everyone else you are likely to meet along the way. Many of us do tend to look at ourselves in isolation, rather than taking a look at the wider picture.

Ask yourself whether or not you have expended most of your energy and concentrated your interest on:

- Caring for ageing parents?
- An all-embracing career that has left you no time for dating?
- Children?
- Grandchildren?
- Bemoaning your fate?

Has your world revolved around any of the above? If the answer is yes to any or all of these questions, then you need to take hold of yourself and look at the world beyond your own small world and expand your horizons. You may think you have a wide general knowledge and insist you always watch the *News* and can discuss any political issue. But what about other human relationships? And how good a listener are you? When you engage in a conversation with a stranger of either sex, do you spend more time listening to what they have to say or interrupting with your own interpretation of events and desperation to get across your own point of view?

On a first date:

Do

- Attempt to find common factors such as children or grandchildren and talk about all the positive aspects of parenting and grandparenting.
- Reveal all the things you've put off until now but still hope to do in the future. It may be that you're hoping to learn abseiling or to take a holiday climbing the Himalayas. Or it may be that you intend to learn Greek. Whatever it is that you've dreamed of, sharing it with your date will really help to sell yourself as an adventurous, positive person; a free spirit with a great *joie de vivre*. One of the greatest blessings of middle age is that often for the first time in your life you have both the time and the money to achieve all those things

you've ever dreamed of. There is nothing more attractive than someone still passionate about something they haven't done yet.

Don't
- Bring up the subject of why you left your ex or why he/she left you, or the reasons for your divorce.
- Moan and groan about the tougher challenges you face alone – although telling a wry story about your own shortcomings can show that you see yourself as an ordinary person and that you're not trying to prove that you're superhuman – it can also show that you have that great sense of humour which appears to be top of every single person's 'must have' list, no matter how old they are.

Be careful that your conversation doesn't give you away as being too staid and rigid. If you admit that you've shopped in Tesco every Thursday afternoon for the last ten years, and say: 'I can't see you on Thursdays because this is a set part of my weekly routine,' what you are actually telling your date is: 'I have a set routine in my life and don't want to change.' If you are going to let someone back into your life, you not only have to be flexible but be willing to prove it.

There are times when silence truly is golden. Never *reveal your entire past to a complete stranger in the two or three hours you are together.* Be *prepared to listen.* Don't *do all the talking and monopolise a conversation.*

Decoding body language

So you've met someone. You're sitting having a drink, a meal or coffee with your new date. You like this person. Conversation is easy. You're deeply engrossed, but this is where body language and active listening come into play. Says Jeremy Milne: 'Always show general interest in the person you're with and in what they are saying. Use active signals such as looking directly into their eyes and maintaining eye contact. Don't be afraid to interject with little interruptions rephrasing a small section of what the other person has said to prove you've been listening and taking it in. This will make your date feel both special and important. Don't be scared to exhibit your sense of humour. That is not to suggest that you embark on a ream of silly jokes, but just add a touch of humour to your general conversation and you will be telling your date that not only do you know who you are and where you are going, but also that you have acquired the great gift of laughing at yourself. When you are middle-aged or older, your conversation and listening skills can sell you as a person.'

You really like this person – but how can you be sure that you're giving off the right signals, and is there any way of letting them know you are interested without actually using the words? How can you be sure that they're interested in you?

According to John Mole, a British body language specialist currently working in the USA, people show they are interested if:

• They lean forward as they listen to you.
• They open their arms and hands as they reply.
• They make lots of eye contact.
• They blink frequently.
• They smile.
• Their feet beneath a table or chair are in the 'sprint' position, balanced on toes.
• Constantly nodding in agreement.

If they are bored by your company they will:

• Sit staring into space.
• Slump.
• Sit jiggling or tapping their feet.

And they will signal the need to get away by:

- Sitting or moving backwards.
- Folding arms or crossing legs.
- Looking around.
- Buttoning or unbuttoning a jacket or coat.

Learn body language and use it as a skill. You may never have met this person before, but watch them closely and you will be able to read their response to you. Watch your own body language. Make sure the signals you are sending are the ones you want to send.

Flirting

Flirting matters. Whether you are eighteen or eighty, flashing those eyelashes, wiggling the hips, making slightly risqué jokes and generally showing that you're attracted as well as attractive is important. But there's a lot more to flirting than merely blinking a few times in the right direction. Flirting is a real art. Peta Heskell, founder of the Flirting Academy (yes there really is such a place – take a look at her website on www.flirtcoach. com) and author of *The Flirt Coach's Guide to Finding the Love You Want*, believes that we're all natural flirts, but many of us have never been encouraged to develop the skills or have simply forgotten how to flirt well. Heskell advises many clients in their forties and fifties who have just come out of a long relationship and sense that flirting is an essential part of the mating process. Most of them hold the view that married people don't flirt. Not only have they lost the skill of flirting but they've also lost the confidence and sense of fun that make a good flirt. But, as Heskell explains, flirting is fun. It's sexy and it's good for you. She encourages people to flirt with everyone they meet, turning up the sexual side of flirting when it's appropriate.

Flirting with the right person can open whole new vistas of

friendship, if nothing more. 'Great flirts create an aura that invites others to share in whatever it is they radiate,' Heskell says. 'People flirt to show they are interested in connecting but you must be prepared both to give out and to receive the flirting message.'

So there you are, out in the 'market place', ready to go. And there are a number of opening plaudits you can use to attract someone you fancy. Remember, however, that before you can reawaken the art of flirting, you have to learn to like who you are and believe you are attractive and desirable.

1. Use your eyes to play 'come hither'. Practise timings. One second of eye contact is often quite enough. Ask your friends to be guinea pigs, practising looking and looking away and back again until it's second nature.
2. Give everyone you meet a sunshine smile, just for fun. Imagine a bright sun in your solar plexus and that each time you smile at someone, they are getting a warm ray from you.
3. Get yourself noticed. Wear something or carry something unusual or even outrageous such as a brooch, ring, tie or outfit that represents you (a flirting prop) that can become the opening subject of a conversation.
4. Don't flirt sexually with someone if that's not the message you want to send. Imagine you have a pilot light of sexuality. It's always burning because you are a sexual being and when it's turned down low, your flirting appears warm and friendly and when you want to take it further, you turn up the flame of desire and flirt sexually.
5. Offer genuine compliments. Don't go over the top with dated 'lines'. Everyone has something great about them. Notice it and tell them about it.
6. Get people to talk about what they love doing. Ask what they're passionate about and listen, repeating words they use often. They will feel important and flattered and happy to be in your company.
7. Use your voice. The voice-eye combination is your top

flirting tool. Vary the tone, pitch and pace of your speech. Listen to the radio and pay attention to the voices of presenters and their guests. What makes them sound 'nice' and 'attractive' to you? Think Sean Connery and Mariella Frostrup and practise changing your voice. If in doubt, ask friends to give you feedback on your voice.

8. When you go to an event, instead of thinking, 'Ooh. All these people, and I'm on my own' think, 'Ooh, people! How exciting!' Don't leave because there are no 'decent, available men or women'. Chat to other people of your own sex. Married and partnered couples are always anxious to fix up single friends and you never know who you might meet at the dinner party, wine tasting or bridge evening your new friends invite you to.

9. Remember, most people ensconced in cosy twosome chats at a party are often talking to the friend they came with. They're probably waiting for someone to break into their chat so they can meet someone new. No one really wants to spend a party talking to someone they see on a regular basis. Stand by the drinks table and say 'Hi' to people who approach. Sometimes it pays off to go up to people with a big, flirtatious smile, introduce yourself and ask, 'And who are you?'

Men should:

- Know what they want and what it is reasonable to expect. Don't expect sex in return for a drink or a meal. When you offer to buy a woman a drink or dinner, accept that this is *all* you are buying. You choose to offer it, without strings.
- Keep your distance. Some men get too close, even when they're only engaging in a casual conversation. Take your approach slowly and look out for little signals like eyes narrowing or a slight movement of the head, backwards. These are signals which say: 'You are invading my space.'
- Touching can be a lovely, flirty action if you are good at

recognising who is a 'touchy feely' sort and who isn't. If you feel the urge to touch, try reaching out, but not actually touching. Pay attention to other people's body language. If they pull away, they are probably not ready for touching yet. If they seem to be OK with it, move on to the next stage.

- Start by touching arms or hands or even a little pat on the back. Never touch a woman you don't know on her bare skin and avoid 'erogenous zones' like her neck and cheeks. It may be seen as an invasion of privacy.

- Don't do the rounds of a group of women, making the same gestures until you find one you think might respond. No woman wants to feel like second, third or even fourth best.

- Only ask for a phone number if you intend to use it. If you sense she's unwilling to offer her number to you, try offering her yours so she can make the first move if she's interested.

Women should:

- Be interesting by being interested. Cut down the 'I am' talk, which is often a nervous habit. Sit back, take a deep breath, make eye contact and ask questions. Throw in a few anecdotes of your own and let the ratio be about 60 per cent listening and 40 per cent talking. Then allow him his turn. Check out whether or not he's following the same rules and is just as anxious to find out about you.

- Be prepared to make a first move. Times have changed and it's OK to approach a guy. You don't have to ask him for a date, but you can hand him your phone number or ask for his email address and then send a message that shows you'd welcome a call from him. As you hand it over, make sure he has to get closer by lowering your voice. Then smile and pull it back a little so he has to move forward to take it. Doing this will tease him, show him he can make the approach and it will also make you aware of how much courage men need to make a first approach.

- Give your real phone number (offer a mobile number rather than a land-line number if you're worried) but don't offer the number of the local Chinese takeaway. Maybe carry a personal card with your name and a mobile number on it.
- Only give out signals for as far as you are really prepared to go. If you start telling dirty jokes to the man you've just met, you could find yourself having to fight off the advances of someone you don't fancy at all.

Peta Heskell adds: 'If you are going to expose acres of bosom and yards of leg, then accept that men will be excited by this and will stare. If you don't like the stares, cover up. There'll be plenty of time for the sexy taunting clothing when you've established a sensual, sexual relationship.'

Who pays?

It's the perennial question. In the sixties and seventies it was fair to share payments if you were both students. Times and etiquette have changed. Slightly older gentlemen, those in their late fifties and sixties, may well expect to pay the bill when they invite a lady out. If she's clearly in a better financial position than he is, then it's fair to expect to share and share alike. I don't believe women should pay to take men out and foot the entire bill unless it's for a special birthday or congratulations celebration. I believe that the guidelines should be based on who issued the invitation in the first place. It may also depend on cost and on venue.

- If he's asked her for a drink or coffee: then it is reasonable for the woman to expect him to pay. If he insists on splitting the bill over little more than a glass of wine, he's too mean to bother dating again.
- If she's invited him for a drink: it is still reasonable to let a man keep his pride and pay for a round or two in a wine bar

or pub, although she may well offer to pay for one round too.

- If he's invited her for a meal in a local restaurant: it might be useful to sort out who pays what before you embark on the outing. A woman might say 'Let's go Dutch' and see the gentleman's reaction. At least that way she knows what to expect. I personally would never second-date a man who not only accepts but then tots up who's had what and expects the woman literally to pay for herself. I don't trust men who keep their change in purses, either!

- If he's invited her to an expensive restaurant: then it's up to her to let it be known she expects him to treat her to the date, especially if it's out of her price range. She might say something along the lines of: 'I've been longing to go there but my pay packet just won't stretch that far.' That way, both know where they are.

- If she has tickets for an event and offers him one: then it's unreasonable to expect him to pay her back – but a real gentleman will offer.

When he insists on treating her to meals and outings and refuses to take payment, then it can be fun to arrange a prepaid treat for him to show that what he's doing isn't taken for granted.

8

Making it work

Falling in love mid-life can be a wonderful, deeply satisfying and altogether perilous experience. When you were young, being loved and being in love filled you with confidence, but by the time you hit forty, you've probably loved several times. The fact that you are now alone means that either you've fallen out of love more than once, been bereaved, or it's all gone terribly wrong.

If you are dating someone regularly, you are probably considering letting them get close to you, both physically and emotionally. Yet, at this mid-life stage, when you may have been involved in several major relationships during your life which either failed, or ended when you didn't want them to, one of the most common questions you may be asking yourself is 'How can I trust again?'

Of course, the object of dating mid-life is to stop dating. You really want to find someone who captures your full attention. No one who wants to fall in love in their forties, fifties or sixties wants to think about having to look for love again. There is, of course, something ultimately reassuring about knowing you have created a 'freestanding' life for yourself. You don't *need* to lean on anyone else to find satisfaction with the way things are. But having found someone you want to get close to and share your life with, how can you be sure that the relationship won't wane? There are no guarantees you won't be let down again. But there are a number of things you *can* do to keep the relationship fresh and exciting. It's easier mid-life than in former years, because you have all the benefit of experience at your fingertips. And I am sure that the key for a successful new relationship in mid-life should be the 'Big Ts' – and also the 'Big Tease'.

The Big Ts

Trust
Tenderness
Tolerance
Togetherness
Thoughtfulness

Trust

must be an implicit part of the new relationship equation. Trusting another person more than you trust yourself is the definition of naïveté. In mid-life, you have to develop your own judgement and honour it above the wishes of others. Learn to listen to your intuition. Don't dismiss it. When you are dating, you usually have good or bad feelings about something or someone. Never brush those feelings aside. Trust them. On the other hand, if you spend every moment you're apart wondering what the other partner is up to, can't bear the thought of your new partner spending time or exchanging conversation with a member of the opposite sex or fear that the attraction you hold is not strong enough to overcome any temptation, then the relationship is doomed from the start.

Tenderness

is a vital component to any relationship, new or old. Tenderness is softness of mind, body and spirit. It's loving, it's cherishing, it's laughing and crying together. It's making love with your eyes, your voice and your body language as much in the middle of a crowded room as well as in the privacy of the bedroom. It's showing by your actions just how much you really do care, not only about your partner, but about those who matter to them. Elderly parents and children (of all ages) who may be trying to come to terms with the end of their parents' marriage need to be taken into consideration as part of the mid-life love package. Many women who have cared for their children from birth face the 'empty nest syndrome', just as they find new partners.

Tolerance

means accepting that you have matured in different worlds and you will almost certainly bring quite different values into the new relationship as well as shared ideals. It's important to remember that when you fall in love as a teenager or twenty-something, or even in your early thirties, you are malleable. You adapt to a new relationship slowly. You learn from one another as time goes by and, gradually, you grow together to form a family unit. But, however young you feel, when you meet someone you intend to spend the rest of your life with mid-life, you don't have the years, or indeed the mind-set, to spend a long period adapting and melding in quite the same way. That's why you need an extra helping of tolerance to accept and understand the modus vivendi of your new partner.

Togetherness

means spending quality time in one another's company as a matter of choice, whether pursuing hobbies or simply chilling out together in comfortable silence. It means being able to communicate your joint pleasure in one another's company. It does not mean spending every hour of every day together. By taking time out to enjoy those pursuits your partner may not necessarily share, your togetherness will become ever more precious. Try to give yourself space to be separate so that when you come together, you do so with renewed pleasure. Book a 'date' with your new partner to do something you enjoyed together when you first met. The time you spend together will become more intimate, and much more fun.

Thoughtfulness

means understanding the pressures and stresses that may beset your new partner and trying to help him or her overcome the difficulties he or she faces, and which may be exaggerated or complicated by this new relationship. It means expecting that things may not always go smoothly and that whatever pressures you face, your partner may be facing similar outside pressures in his or her own way, too. Create opportunities for little surprises. It may be nothing more than a small, inexpensive posy of flowers offered for no good reason; a favourite food that appears on the table to tantalise taste or a small deed done to add to your partner's comfort or pleasure. Of course every relationship becomes more comfortable as it matures. But never permit it to become too comfortable. Shabby old slippers may feel good, but they look awful. You can find new slippers that are comfortable, too. It's vital to keep surprise alive to ensure an enduring relationship.

The Big Tease

The Big Tease is as important as the Big Ts. As I said earlier, active sexual relationships can be as vital to health as a nutritionally well-balanced diet. Giving intimate physical pleasure to your partner is perhaps the greatest gift of all.

How to handle new sex when you're older

You're never too old to enjoy lovemaking. Spontaneity is perhaps the most endearing feature of all when it comes to kindling a new love and keeping the flame of love on fire. Why would your partner think of looking elsewhere when they've got exciting, enticing, sexy you? And it's been proved that boring, unsatisfying sex is one of the major causes of relationship breakdowns. If you've cooked your partner a marvellous meal, or treated them to one in a wonderful restaurant and then sat watching them as they licked their lips after the last morsel, the stresses and strains of the world seemed a million miles away. Sex can be like that. Liplickingly wonderful. And like a recipe that's been practised and improved on many times, it can improve with time as the relationship sets and gels. As you learn how to give your partner the special pleasures they enjoy most, so they will learn to pleasure you. Here are a few tricks which might help keep your relationship as fresh in the future as at the beginning:

- Give yourself time to become intimate with one another. Go for a long walk, hand-in-hand. Take turns massaging or pampering one another. Treat yourself to some luxury body lotions or shower gels and sexy new undies and nightwear. Don't do it just once. Do it regularly if you want to continue to have fun with your new mate. There's nothing more off-putting than grey bras and baggy Y-fronts.
- When you've been celibate for some time, your desire for one another may take you by surprise. Be ready to explore one another gently. But don't be scared of a surprising, urgent passion of a kind that may not have overtaken you in years. Let it happen. Enjoy it. Don't let it scare you.
- Be prepared to experiment with a new partner. If they suggest something you've never tried before, give it a go. Try showering or bathing together. You may be in your forties, fifties or sixties, but if you're a self-confessed chocoholic or

ice-cream addict, take some of your partner's favourite tastes to the bedroom and give them a lick-smacking massage.
- Excite one another by reading from sexy books or magazines.
- Let your lovemaking be as varied and exciting as you can make it. You can lead by being gentle and loving, comfortable and mind-blowingly sexy by turns. You may not have the body of a teenager any more, but invest in sexy nightwear or undies. Nurture this new relationship with exciting loving. Try it in rooms other than the bedroom. Being older doesn't prohibit you from playing and having real fun.

Be friends first

Whether you're freshly footloose and fancy-free or have been without a relationship for some time, readjusting to a new relationship is not easy in mid-life when you've already established a pattern to your life and expect your day-to-day routine to follow a certain route. I believe that when you're young, physical chemistry often overrides liking and friendship. However, I think that when you look for a partner later in life, you need to find real friendship too. You need to be what love guru Shmuley Boteach describes as 'in like' before you can be truly 'in love'. Compromise and compatibility are two key words in any new mid-life relationship. Compatibility is obvious, but compromise is probably one of the hardest issues to come to terms with when you've become used to putting yourself first, as inevitably you do when you're used to being alone. I know from experience.

When Peter and I first embarked on our relationship, I found it incredibly difficult to use the 'we' word when I was so used to being just 'I'. On paper 'we' both enjoy music. My taste is for eclectic modern classical, particularly the big band sounds. His is for true classical and operatic works of Beethoven, Mozart and Bizet. We compromise. I've found I love going to light opera; he's begun to accept and enjoy my CD collection and adds to it on a regular basis. I'm obsessively tidy. My insistence on putting everything away drives him mad at times. He prefers to live in organised chaos. We compromise. He has his office, and if he leaves papers everywhere in his own space, I've learned to close the door – as long as he doesn't encroach and mess up our mutual living areas. Desperate to assert my newly discovered independence, I insisted on performing all manner of minor household repairs at the beginning of our relationship; skills acquired during my years alone. But I also accept that Peter can often mend, make and decorate far faster and more efficiently than I can. He's had to learn to give me credit for knowing what to do; I've had to learn that it's OK to ask for his help. He's a gadget-addict; I'm a born Luddite. I'm learning that gadgets can be fun; he's learning not to waste money on nonsense. Between us, we've learned how to compromise to our mutual advantage. It's taken a long time for us to reach our present happy live-and-let-live status. But I have to say that I for one feel more content and emotionally secure than I did on our wedding day. From the start, both of us were (and still are) aware that fitting two middle-aged halves together into a single, cohesive partnership is not easy. The one quality that has helped more than any other is that we share a similar sense of humour.

Open a new chapter

When you go dating with someone you really like/fancy do remember: you are opening a new page in your life; this is a new relationship; the person you are with knows nothing about you, except what you have told them.

Do:

- Talk to one another about the things that matter most to you.
- Be ready to try and enjoy new experiences.

- Be prepared to make mistakes.
- Be prepared to admit mistakes.
- Let down your guard and be yourself.

Don't

- Expect to share a history you don't have.
- Expect your new partner to second-guess your desires/needs at the beginning of the relationship. They need time to learn about the real 'you'.
- Embark on a relationship talking about people your date doesn't know, places he/she has no interest in, or discussing the details of a former relationship.
- Go on about your past. Comparisons are odious. This is a new relationship, enjoy it for itself.

My own examples of the small adjustments we have made may sound unimportant and in some ways inconsequential – but even the smallest irritations grow bigger if left to fester. Forty per cent of first marriages ended in divorce in Britain in 2000, according to the Office of Statistics, but an astounding *75 per cent* of all second marriages fail. This is because many people rush into a second marriage without thinking about all the implications, and the situation is further complicated because children (of any age) from a first marriage can be very resentful of a new partner in your life.

Are you certain?

'There is nothing more certain than uncertainties; fortune is full of fresh variety; constant is nothing but inconstancy.' So wrote poet Richard Barnfield almost four hundred years ago. And how right he was. Of course, no one is ever 100 per cent certain about anything. Life is a gamble, but you can increase the likelihood of success, of course.

Before you make a commitment, ask yourself:

1. Do I really *like* this person? Yes ❑ No ❑
2. Can I really put up with their small irritations and quirky behaviour? Yes ❑ No ❑
3. Do I think they will be able to put up with my foibles in the long term? Yes ❑ No ❑
4. Am I ready to relinquish some of my independence in the cause of this new relationship? Yes ❑ No ❑
5. Am I ready to share most areas of my life? Yes ❑ No ❑
6. Can I warmly and wholeheartedly welcome other people such as elderly parents or recalcitrant teenagers, or possibly even step-grandchildren into my family circle and am I sure that my partner will do the same? Yes ❑ No ❑
7. Will I be able to adapt new standards of living and life-style that will inevitably be part of the relationship? Yes ❑ No ❑
8. Will my existing family react well to the idea of sharing me? Yes ❑ No ❑
9. Is their acceptance of my new status and the husband or wife of someone who is not their parent important to me? Yes ❑ No ❑
10. Will my new partnership affect my financial status? (If so, how? No matter how much I trust my new partner, should I make legal arrangements to guard my assets?) Yes ❑ No ❑

If you can't answer at least eight of the above ten questions positively (and for your own sake, do be honest), then this may not be the fully committed relationship you are hoping for – yet.

Laying the baggage aside

By the time we reach mid-life, we all have 'baggage'. One of the hardest tasks you will face is learning to offload it on to a trolley of memories. People who tell you to 'forget it' are being unrealistic. It's not easy to shed deeply ingrained fears and sorrows born of a previous experience. Children will serve as permanent reminders of a previous life, and so they should. But you can learn to lay aside the pain and hurt that may have dogged a former relationship and allow yourself to build a new, fresh life. Only when you've managed to do that will you be ready to move on.

Steps to moving on

1. Are you in the same home that you shared with a previous spouse or partner? If so, are you prepared to move?
2. If you are bereaved, is your home a 'shrine' to your lost partner? If you are divorced, is your garage or other storage space still stuffed with memorabilia of a previous life that you no longer want but can't bear to part with?

If the answer to either of these question is yes, then you may need to rethink your priorities. If you want to make a new relationship work, you have to drop certain physical reminders of your former life. If you can't do it alone, don't be scared to ask for help. It could be the best investment you ever make. It's an investment in your future happiness.

Accepting help

Determination to succeed in your quest for a new partner is half the battle. However, when a relationship begins from scratch at a time when you've already graduated from the University of Life, and when the few low marks you have achieved seem to have left more of an indent on your soul than the far more prestigious and numerous highpoints you scored, you may well need to offload some of the baggage you've collected along the way. There's no shame in seeking help to clean your palate before you try tasting a new relationship. If you're having trouble building relationships, or maintaining them, then it may be well worthwhile to consider counselling. Being sure of yourself and your own worth is desperately important. If you believe in yourself and your own worth, then so will others. The British Association for Counselling and Psychotherapy based in Rugby in Warwickshire has lists of accredited specialist counsellors all over Britain who will help you. Few counsellors are free (as BACP's Press Officer, therapist Dr Philip Hodson, explains: 'Counsellors have to eat too'), but free help is available on the National Health Service through 60 per cent of British doctors surgeries. You may find reasonably priced counselling available through training centres such as the Tavistock Clinic in London or the London Centre for Psychotherapy. BACP carry a full list of therapists and training centres where reasonably priced and well-supervised therapy may be offered as part of the training programme. Relationship therapy is widely available throughout the USA, too. Every state has a list of licensed and qualified therapists, and they and their specialities are listed in local libraries, in yellow page directories or via the Internet.

Location – his home or hers?

When you embark on a new, and hopefully long-term relationship, you will need to make a number of life-changing decisions. Among them is: his place or hers?

I didn't face the problem of sharing an old home with a new spouse because I had already moved out of the former marital home by the time Peter and I met – but I know several people who did, including my own dad. It can never be easy for a new partner to move into a home that was once shared by your partner and someone else, and find yourself surrounded by carpets, furniture and pictures she chose, books she read, kitchen utensils she used etc. I know my adopted mother bitterly resented living in my own mother's home. And I think she had every right to feel so. I don't know why my father chose to stay. For the most part, those who stay, do so because moving is a financially impractical option. If this is what you *both* decide on:

- Choose a new bed together.
- Invest in new bedding and linen.
- Clear out clothes, toiletries and all other personal items before your new partner takes up residence.
- Decorate and refurbish as much as you can.
- Encourage your new partner to bring their artwork and cherished knick-knacks along so that they feel they're at home.

All this may sound very obvious, but I know one couple who moved into 'his' house after their wedding. To her dismay, the new wife opened the wardrobe to find it still filled with her dead predecessor's clothes. If you're the one moving in, DO insist you reconnoitre your new living quarters before you take up residence. If there are things around which you feel ought not to be there, say so, and demand that they're moved. *Don't feel embarrassed. Be firm.* There are a few exceptions to this rule:

- Women may want their own familiar cooking implements and pans because they're comfortable to work with and not because they are souvenirs of an old relationship. That is as reasonable as a man hanging on to his own tool box and drill. It's not hoarding!
- Most couples I know where one or both partners have suffered a bereavement also like to have one old 'family' photograph around, showing them with their first spouse and family. This encourages the children's acceptance of the new relationship. Their late parent may be gone, but you still remember the love and closeness you once all shared as a family. A new partner's acceptance of this photograph can really help towards gelling the new family with the old. I know it can often be hard for a partner, particularly a divorcee

or one who has never been married before, to accept a single photograph on display, but this is one area of acceptance which can only serve to enhance the new relationship.

Jealousy

Embarking on a new relationship will mean learning to accept new values and new ground rules. I believe the most important of these is giving one another emotional, psychological and physical space.

Do you:

1. Question every moment they *don't* spend with you?
2. Find it hard to understand why he/she wants to spend time without you in the company of their own family (possibly parents as well as children)?
3. Expect this new partner to follow the same behavioural patterns as a previous partner?
4. Think about your new partner's needs and put them first, or feel your own needs are paramount in this relationship?

If you or your new partner have spent time alone, then it's only reasonable to expect each other to want and respect the need for a certain amount of privacy and freedom – not only of time, but of physical space, too.

In a first marriage, the parents of one partner will very likely have, over the years, grown to accept the other partner as a loved and loving member of their family. This emotion may well endure long after the marriage is over. The parents may want to continue their relationship with the former partner. Moreover, the parents of the former partner will want to continue their relationship with their grandchildren. Respecting everyone's wishes may not be easy. But it is essential if the new relationship is to endure.

Your children

In a first marriage or relationship, a couple generally get to know each other before children appear on the scene. In a second or subsequent relationship, the children appear first, and may come as part of the package with a new partner. They will expect and (in my opinion) have the right to a certain priority with their own parent at times, especially if they are still living in, or regularly visiting, the new marital home.

Getting the priorities right

Every relationship expert I know will tell you that you need to put your partner first and your children second in any relationship. Too many marriages founder because when children appear, one partner, generally the mother, insists on putting their needs and desires above all else. This applies just as much in a second or subsequent marriage, but be careful.

When you've got children, and regardless of their age, they need to know that despite the new relationship, they're still a priority in your life. However, while it's important to listen to them and respect their views, they should not be allowed to wreck your chances of happiness because they don't approve of your relationship. Listen to them. Hear what they have to say. But remember, you have a right to a life, too.

- Encourage stepchildren to feel 'at home' and don't feel 'put-upon' if they walk into the house and raid your fridge or help themselves to your drinks. 'Your' is now 'our' – so take it as a compliment.
- Try not to blame your partner if children show openly (or furtively) that they resent the relationship. More anguish can be caused in a relationship by dissenting and disapproving children than by almost any other outside influence.

- Don't work too hard at the step-parenting role. Let the children come to you, rather than making over-generous gestures towards them, which might be misinterpreted.
- Never try to 'displace' a parent, whether living or dead, in your step-offspring's eyes. That is not only cruel but also futile. Remember, they will always be 'steps', even if they're quite small when you take them on.

Remember, your children are not your partners' children. Endeavour to treat all offspring (including grandchildren and step-grandchildren) exactly the same way as you do your own. It's not always easy, given that different families have different patterns of accepted behaviour. There are times when I do something naturally with my own daughters which my stepsons think odd. Conversely, the same happens with Peter and his sons. This could be the difference between having sons and daughters, though as I don't have sons of my own (and am certainly never likely to now), I'll never know. Play family rules the way they're played by their own family. Be prepared to let your partner take the lead with their own children. It can be difficult. Sometimes, you may be forced to behave in a way which feels alien. But do it, and you'll save much grief. If you show that you resent time spent with an existing family, and that you feel excluded, you're storing up a hornet's nest full of trouble. You might, however, avert showdowns by talking it through and deciding who does what with whom. If there is obviously outright opposition to you, and even if it's painful, stay away!

Once again, jealousy of old relationships viz new ones can become a major source of contention, especially if the step-parent feels that the parent is offering their offspring emotional or material support they feel should now be theirs, or vice versa. As the child of just such a relationship, as well as the parent within one, I know just how important it is for children of any age to spend time alone with their parents as well as time together as part of a re-constituted family. I also know the tightrope the parent walks if the new partner feels 'left out' of the family deal. My mother died when I was a small, only child. Inevitably, I was upstairs doing homework when my father got home from work. He used to rush in, by-pass my adoptive mother, his second wife, yelling all the way up the stairs: 'Where's my Andrea?' when what he should have done was to have greeted her first, kissed her, acknowledged her presence, and *then* come upstairs to see me. My adoptive mother was understandably terribly jealous of my relationship with him. It soured our relationship for many years. I couldn't understand why she resented me so much when I tried so hard to please her. As an adult in a similar situation (although with much older offspring), I'm still aware of the unnecessary animosity my father's albeit innocent actions caused between my adoptive mother and I. Of course, it is vital that children of any age from one liaison should be made to feel as treasured as ever they were even within a step-parental relationship, but not at the expense of a new partner's feelings.

Be generous enough to permit your partner the right to enjoy time out with his or her children alone from the outset if they want to and you will merit a great deal of respect and admiration from both partner and children. If you guard the child (or new partner) too closely, you will build up justifiable resentment between them which, in turn, will affect your relationship with one another.

Money

Sort out all finances *before* you meet the registrar. Who will be responsible for which utility bills, or will you split them? Will you halve the cost of holidays? Money can be a bone of contention if children think a new partner is about to eat into their 'inheritance'. If you buy a joint property, who will be entitled to what in the event of death or divorce? Make sure that you register any property you buy together with joint funds as 'tenants in common', and stick to a few basic rules with the Land Registry. If one of you moves into a property already owned by the other, will you give your new spouse a legal undertaking that they have a home for life, even if it is eventually to pass to your children? Make wills which may not necessarily be back-to-back this time round. Ask a solicitor to draw up a prenuptial agreement that suits you both. Pension policies are a minefield, particularly where there are former partners. Make sure that your intentions are cut and dried so that there will be no arguments as to your wishes after your death. Discuss your intentions with other members of the family, including your children, so that they know exactly where they stand. You may elicit the same response that I have done: 'Oh Mother! I don't want to know!' The sewing table in our hallway, which belongs to my husband, has become a standing joke between my youngest stepson and I. But equally, and for their sakes, you need to make sure that they *do* know what is yours and what is theirs. A family meeting with all sides present is a good idea and then there can be no misunderstanding. You may not have a fortune and although such agreements have no legal standing, solicitors can use them as a declaration of intent if there are any arguments after your death or that of your partner.

Ten top tips to secure your future together

Guarding and fostering a new relationship is rather like maintaining a car. When it's new, you may guard it cautiously for the first few weeks. You take it out and start spinning it around, showing it off to anyone prepared to look. But then you begin to take it for granted. You may park it on yellow lines, spill drinks on the seats, forget to have it cleaned or serviced. The car may run if you treat it thus, but bet your bottom dollar it won't run as efficiently as it did when you first became the proud new owner. Partnerships are no different. Take a new partner for granted as the weeks become months and years, and although the association may endure, it will become stale and unexciting and you'll end up either desperately unhappy, bored, or just another statistic!

It doesn't matter how old you are, love is a complex emotion. It is physical, chemical and biological. It requires trust, respect and plenty of communication to help it flourish and endure. You may have worked hard in order to find the person with whom you can exchange those three, magical little words 'I love you', but that's not the end. It's just the beginning.

Rule 1: keep on courting

Whatever it was that attracted you and your partner to one another and caused you to make a commitment of any kind is worth repeating. Never take love for granted. Continue to treat one another as you did on the day you first met. Little messages that say 'I love you' left on a pillow say as much as any jewels. So do messages such as 'I miss you' if you're apart. The sum of tiny gestures of love is greater than all its parts.

Rule 2: share responsibilities and control

You may have been forced to act independently for years. You may be used to making all your own rules. Resist the urge to play leader or follow-my-leader all the time. Romance needs energy and input from you both. Make joint decisions. Never be scared to add your input or point of view, but don't try to run the show alone.

Rule 3: focus on common interests

Work and other family responsibilities can often dominate everyday life without us realising what's happening. When two people come together mid-life, there are already so many calls on our time that we may find it hard to find the time to share the things that give us both the greatest pleasure. Plan in advance to do the things you enjoy together. You both love concerts – then book tickets. You love walking or cycling –

then cross out an hour or two in your own and your partners' diaries. Don't talk about it. Do it. Mid-life, life's too short to waste time. Be ready to tune in to your partner when you are together. Be observant. Be attentive. Listen to what they are saying. A good relationship means sharing joys and worries and helping to solve fears and concerns when you can. If your partner needs to let off steam, you don't need to offer a solution, just be there to listen. Make the time you spend together quality time.

Rule 4: time spent apart
Enrol for an evening class that interests you. Continue to enjoy a hobby you've always enjoyed alone. Even short absences make the time you spend together more precious.

Rule 5: learn something new together
Take lessons, enrol for a class or participate in an adventure which involves embarking on something new for both of you. It may be hang-gliding or painting or perhaps you've always wanted to learn how to sail. Whatever it is, invest in building a new future together.

Rule 6: don't harbour grudges
Forget about 'never going to bed angry'. Going to bed angry gives you cooling off time. You go to sleep angry. You awake next morning and discover you can't remember what made you so cross the night before. So you turn over, cuddle up and use the surge of hormones that rose with the emotion of anger to make love instead. It's a great way to resolve an argument and could cement the relationship even further.

Rule 7: write one another love letters
It may be that email has superseded the old-fashioned letter where business is concerned, but there's nothing as wonderful as having a handwritten love note you can take out of a drawer and read over and over again. Remember the joy of your teenage

days when you received a love letter. Rekindle the magic. Handwritten letters, which say just what's in your heart, and little poems (who cares if they don't scan?) created just for your loved one can be intensely precious. If your handwriting's unreadable, print them out. It's the effort that makes them worth so much.

Rule 8: establish family traditions

Agree that you will celebrate an anniversary and every month go out that day for a special celebration. Make new birthday traditions come alive, perhaps by making sure that there's always a cake, or by inviting all sides of your new, whole family for a get-together. Is there a piece of music you can adopt as your own, to be played whenever you're asked for your favourite tune because it reminds you of a special time spent together? Or special flowers which have a joint meaning? Women CAN send men flowers. Why not? Create moments that are meaningful to you as a couple. You are never too old for real romance.

Rule 9: practise good health

You may promise to live in sickness and in health and mean it, but health is better. Work out together, or swim or go walking. Eat healthily. And if you do get the odd aches and pains that come with age, don't wallow in them. Empathise, and try to ease them away.

Rule 10: keep talking

The more you talk to your partner, the closer you will become. Talk politics. Talk sport. Talk children. Talk friends. Talk interests. Share your deepest thoughts, your innermost emotions with the person you love.

Now you've found one another, where's the rush?

I know a number of over-forties who've met a potential partner and, within a week or two, they've set the wedding date! I've never been able to understand why. When you make any major purchase, you give it careful consideration. It's a big investment and you give it the respect of time because you know that what you are doing may have a long-term effect on the rest of your life. And can there be any more important decision than a lifetime partnership?

When you meet someone mid-life, there's no ticking time clock. If you're unlikely to want to start a family, where's the rush to make a commitment? Far better to take it slowly, and get to know one another properly before you commit yourself to any kind of long-term relationship, and that includes moving in together. If you meet someone and you care deeply for one another, you may well want commitment eventually. I did. Peter and I dated for five years before we committed to one another with a marriage licence. It was a matter of dotting the I's, crossing the T's and ensuring that both of us were going into a new relationship with our eyes wide open. I don't regret one day of those five years.

If you wake up every morning from the first day on, believing that this is the first day of a whole new relationship, you will know for sure that you have found your mid-life love.

Useful contacts

Counselling advice

British Association for Counselling and Psychotherapy
1 Regent Place
Rugby
Warwickshire CV21 2PJ

Tel: 0870 443 5252

Internet dating sites

Christian Dating Site
www.christianconnection.co.uk

Jewish Dating Channel
www.totallyjewish.com

Love and Friends
www.loveandfriends.com

Dating Direct
www.datingdirect.com

uDate
www.udate.com

Mature Internet dating site

Cyber suitors
www.cybersuitors.com

Introduction agencies and contacts

Association of British Introduction Agencies
35 Market Street
Tamworth
Staffs B19 7LR

Tel: 0845 345 ABIA or 0845 345 2242
Email: enquiries@abia.org.uk
Website: www.abia.org.uk

Autumn Friends and Woodland Friends
Tel: 01874 636 909
Website: justwoodlandfriends.com

Whichintro
Website containing database of all active introduction agencies
in the UK with details: www.whichintro.com

Safety on the Internet and counselling
www.wiredsafety.org

Social clubs for mature singles

Caring Adults Singles Club Arranging Diverse Events
Rosebanks
The Green
Pilning
South Glos BS35 4QF

Tel: 01454 63 11 44
Website: www.cascade.eu.com

Initial Approach
4 Beech Road
Dunblane FK15 OLA

Tel: 01786 825777
Website: www.initial-approach.co.uk

Nexus Singles
Club Nexus House
6 The Quay
Bideford
North Devon EX39 2HW

Tel: 01237 471 704

Northern Link
Karen Seddon
26 Fryent Close
Blackrod
Bolton BL6 5BU

Tel: 01204 460 989
Website: www.northernlink.co.uk

Speed dating

Speed Daters
Tel: 08702 430 935
Website: www.speeddater.co.uk

TV opportunities

Entertainment jobs and opportunities
Website: www.talent-scouts.org.uk

RDF Media
Website: www.rdfmedia.com

The Dating Channel (Digital TV)
Website: www.thedatingchannel.com

Who Wants To Be On TV
Website: www.whowantstobeontv.co.uk

Others

Single Travellers Action Group
STAG
Church Lane
Sharnbrook
Bedford
Beds MK44 1HR

The Flirt Academy
Tel: 0700 435 4784
Email: info@flirtcoach.com
Website: www.flirtingacademy.com

See also Heskell, Peta, *The Flirt Coach's Guide to Finding the Love You Want* (HarperCollins, 2003)

US singles holidays
Website: www.singlesonthego.com

Index